Braxton Bragg vs. William Rosecrans: The Battles of Stones River (Murfreesboro) and Chickamauga

By Charles River Editors

Rosecrans and Bragg

About Charles River Editors

Charles River Editors was founded by Harvard and MIT alumni to provide superior editing and original writing services, with the expertise to create digital content for publishers across a vast range of subject matter. In addition to providing original digital content for third party publishers, Charles River Editors republishes civilization's greatest literary works, bringing them to a new generation via ebooks.

Introduction

BATTLE OF STONE RIVER

The Battle of Stones River (December 31, 1862-January 2, 1863)

"In all, fifty-eight pieces of artillery played upon the enemy. Not less than one hundred shots per minute were fired. As the mass of men swarmed down the slope they were mowed down by the score. Confederates were pinioned to the earth by falling branches." – G. C. Kniffin, aide to General Crittenden

Americans have long been fascinated by the Civil War and its biggest battles, particularly Gettysburg, Antietam, and Shiloh, all of which involved Robert E. Lee or Ulysses S. Grant. But one of the 6 biggest battles of the war, and the one that took the heaviest toll by % on both armies was fought at the end of 1862 in Tennessee, and it involved neither of those generals.

In late December 1862, William Rosecrans's Union Army of the Cumberland was contesting Middle Tennessee against Braxton Bragg's Army of Tennessee, and for three days the two armies savaged each other as Bragg threw his army at Rosecrans in a series of desperate assaults. Bragg's army was unable to dislodge the Union army, and he eventually withdrew his army after learning that Rosecrans was on the verge of receiving reinforcements. Though the battle was stalemated, the fact that the Union army was left in possession of the field allowed Rosecrans to declare victory and embarrassed Bragg.

Though Stones River is mostly overlooked as a Civil War battle today, it had a decisive impact on the war. The two armies had both suffered nearly 33% casualties, an astounding number in 1862 that also ensured Rosecrans would not start another offensive campaign in Tennessee until the following June. The Union victory also ensured control of Nashville, Middle Tennessee, and Kentucky for the rest of the war, prompting Lincoln to tell Rosecrans, "You gave us a hard-earned victory, which had there been a defeat instead, the nation could scarcely have lived over." The battle and its results also set into motion a chain of events that would lead to Rosecrans and Bragg facing off at the crucial battle of Chickamauga in September 1863, a battle that is often viewed as the last gasp for the Confederates' hopes in the West.

Bragg vs. Rosecrans comprehensively covers the campaign and the events that led up to the battle, the fighting itself, and the aftermath of the battle. Accounts of the battle by important participants are also included, along with maps of the battle and pictures of important people, places, and events. You will learn about the Battle of Stones River like you never have before, in no time at all.

BATTLE OF CHICKAMAUGA

The Battle of Chickamauga (September 19-20, 1863)

"I know Mr. Davis thinks he can do a great many things other men would hesitate to attempt. For instance, he tried to do what God failed to do. He tried to make a soldier of Braxton Bragg." – General Joseph E. Johnston

Americans have long been fascinated by the Civil War and its biggest battles, particularly Gettysburg, Antietam, and Shiloh, all of which involved Robert E. Lee or Ulysses S. Grant. But the second biggest battle of the entire war mostly gets overlooked among casual readers, despite the fact it represented the last great chance for the Confederates to salvage the Western theater.

In mid-September, the Union Army of the Cumberland under General William Rosecrans had taken Chattanooga, but rather than be pushed out of the action, Army of Tennessee commander Braxton Bragg decided to stop with his 60,000 men and prepare a counterattack south of Chattanooga at a creek named Chickamauga. To bolster his fire-power, Confederate President Jefferson Davis sent 12,000 additional troops under the command of Lieutenant General James Longstreet, whose corps had just recently fought at Gettysburg in July.

On the morning of September 19, 1863, Bragg's men assaulted the Union line, which was established in a wooded area thick with underbrush along the river. That day and the morning of the next, Bragg continue to pummel Union forces, with the battle devolving from an organized succession of coordinated assaults into what one Union soldier described as "a mad, irregular battle, very much resembling guerrilla warfare on a vast scale in which one army was bushwhacking the other, and wherein all the science and the art of war went for nothing."

Late that second morning, Rosecrans was misinformed that a gap was forming in his front line, so he responded by moving several units forward to shore it up. What Rosecrans didn't realize, however, was that in doing so he accidentally created a quarter-mile gap in the Union center, directly in the path of Longstreet's men. Described by one of Rosecrans' own men as "an angry flood," Longstreet's attack was successful in driving one-third of the Union Army off the field, with Rosecrans himself running all the way to Chattanooga, where he was later found weeping and seeking solace from a staff priest.

As the Confederate assault continued, George H. Thomas led the Union left wing against heavy Confederate attack even after nearly half of the Union army abandoned their defenses and retreated from the battlefield, racing toward Chattanooga. Thomas rallied the remaining parts of the army and formed a defensive stand on Horseshoe Ridge, with more units spontaneously rallying to the new defensive line. Thomas and his men managed to hold until nightfall, when they made an orderly retreat to Chattanooga while the Confederates occupied the surrounding heights, ultimately besieging the city. Dubbed "The Rock of Chickamauga", Thomas's heroics ensured that Rosecrans' army was able to successfully retreat back to Chattanooga.

In the aftermath of the Battle of Chickamauga, several Confederate generals blamed the number of men lost during what would be the bloodiest battle of the Western Theater on Bragg's incompetence, also criticizing him for refusing to pursue the escaping Union army. General Longstreet later stated to Jefferson Davis, "Nothing but the hand of God can help as long as we have our present commander."

Bragg vs. Rosecrans comprehensively covers the campaign and the events that led up to the battle, the fighting itself, and the aftermath of the battle. Accounts of the battle by important participants are also included, along with maps of the battle and pictures of important people, places, and events. You will learn about the Battle of Chickamauga like you never have before.

The Battle of Stones River

Chapter 1: Middle Tennessee

The most famous battle in the West during the Civil War may have been the Battle of Shiloh, where General Ulysses S. Grant's army barely survived an onslaught against Albert Sidney Johnston's Confederates near the border between Tennessee and Georgia, but the location and result of that battle have often obscured the fact that the Confederates and Federals were desperately contesting the state of Tennessee and Kentucky to the north and east throughout the year.

Johnston's push against Grant had been at the directive of President Jefferson Davis, who wanted his commanders in the West to be aggressive, and in October 1862 Braxton Bragg's Army of Mississippi marched into Kentucky in an attempt to capture that all important border state. At the Battle of Perryville on October 8, Bragg's army defeated a corps from Union commander Don Carlos Buell's Army of the Ohio, but after the battle Bragg retreated back into Tennessee, meeting up with Kirby Smith's 10,000 Confederates and merging forces around Murfreesboro. After some of his men were sent to help garrison Vicksburg on the Mississippi River, Bragg's newly christened Army of Tennessee was about 35,000 strong.

Don Carlos Buell had received much of the credit for the victory at Shiloh in April, and probably undeservedly so, but he has been fiercely criticized for his performance at Perryville after leaving two of his army's corps idle during the battle. In *All for the Regiment*, historian Gerald J. Prokopowicz asserted, "The two other corps of Buell's army were each as large as the entire Confederate force engaged. Had they both advanced boldly once the battle was underway, they could have seized the town of Perryville, cut off the attackers from their supply depots in central Kentucky, and very possibly achieved a decisive battlefield victory on the model of Austerlitz or Waterloo."

When Buell failed to vigorously pursue Bragg's retreating army and decided to stay around Nashville, the impatient Lincoln Administration reorganized the command in that vicinity, creating the Department of the Cumberland under William Rosecrans. With that, Buell's Army of the Ohio became part of a new army led by Rosecrans, the Army of the Cumberland, in late October. Lincoln wanted Rosecrans to quickly lead an offensive against the nearby Confederates and thrust into eastern Tennessee, but Rosecrans had other ideas and insisted in his post-battle report that he needed to reorganize and outfit the army for two months instead:

> "Assuming command of the army at Louisville on October 27, it was found concentrated at Bowling Green and Glasgow, distant about 113 miles from Louisville, from whence, after replenishing with ammunition, supplies, and clothing, they moved on to Nashville, the advance corps reaching that place on the morning of November 7, a distance of 183 miles from Louisville.

At this distance from my base of supplies, the first thing to be done was to provide for the subsistence of the troops and open the Louisville and Nashville Railroad. The cars commenced running through on November 26, previous to which time our supplies had been brought by rail to Mitchellsville, 35 miles north of Nashville, and from thence, by constant labor, we had been able to haul enough to replenish the exhausted stores for the garrison at Nashville and subsist the troops of the moving army.

From November 26 to December 26 every effort was bent to complete the clothing of the army; to provide it with ammunition, and replenish the depot at Nashville with needful supplies; to insure us against want from the largest possible detention likely to occur by the breaking of the Louisville and Nashville Railroad, and to insure this work the road was guarded by a heavy force posted at Gallatin. The enormous superiority in numbers of the rebel cavalry kept our little cavalry force almost within the infantry lines, and gave the enemy control of the entire country around us. It was obvious from the beginning that we should be confronted by Bragg's army, recruited by an inexorable conscription, and aided by clans of mounted men, formed into a guerrilla-like cavalry, to avoid the hardships of conscription and infantry service. The evident difficulties and labors of an advance into this country, and against such a force, and at such distance from our base of operations, with which we were connected but by a single precarious thread, made it manifest that our policy was to induce the enemy to travel over as much as possible of the space that separated us, thus avoiding for us the wear and tear and diminution of our forces, and subjecting the enemy to all this inconvenience, besides increasing for him and diminishing for us the dangerous consequences of a defeat. The means taken to obtain this end were eminently successful. The enemy, expecting us to go into winter quarters at Nashville, had prepared his own winter quarters at Murfreesborough, with the hope of possibly making them at Nashville, and had sent a large cavalry force into West Tennessee to annoy Grant, and another large force into Kentucky to break up the railroad."

As Rosecrans's account suggests, he was reluctant to push forward with an offensive until he was certain his army was ready, and even then he started overestimating the size of Bragg's army near Murfreesboro. For his part, Bragg's post-battle report would claim Rosecrans had 60,000 effectives, when in fact Rosecrans only had about 66% of that. Meanwhile, as Rosecrans was getting everything he felt was necessary around Nashville, Confederate cavalry led by Col. John Hunt Morgan harassed Rosecrans's lines of communication and supply lines around the area, scoring a win at the Battle of Hartsville that only further demoralized the Union.

Rosecrans's hesitation is sometimes viewed as needless dawdling, but his concerns were also understandable given the timing. It was rare for 19th century armies to campaign during the winter months, which made traveling harder, illnesses more likely, and lowered morale due to additional hardships associated with cold weather. Despite that, the Lincoln Administration had to deal with politics, most notably midterm election losses that November, and after feeling like a golden opportunity had been lost at Antietam, Lincoln and his War Department were all that more anxious for a grand push. It would have disastrous results for Ambrose Burnside and the Army of the Potomac against Lee's Army of Northern Virginia in mid-December at the Battle of Fredericksburg, and Rosecrans likely would have waited until spring of 1863 himself if his job wasn't on the line.

As a result, Rosecrans would put his army in motion on the day after Christmas. Of all the commanders who led armies during major battles of the Civil War, historians have by and large agreed that the most inept generals to face each other were Rosecrans and Bragg, and the Stones River campaign would be the first major reason for those harsh assessments.

Chapter 2: Moving to Murfreesboro

Bragg's estimate that Rosecrans had 60,000 effectives may have been accurate had it not failed to account for the fact that Rosecrans would have to leave men around Nashville, and by the time he put his Army of the Cumberland in motion toward Murfreesboro and Bragg's army, he had only about 40,000 men on the move.

On December 26, the three "wings" of the Union army began heading southeast, encountering Joseph Wheeler's Confederate cavalry from nearly the beginning. With Union cavalry screening the movements, Major General Thomas Crittenden's left wing, which included divisions led by Generals Thomas Wood, John Palmer, and Horatio Van Cleve, began marching along the Nashville and Chattanooga Railroad. Major General Alexander McCook, which included divisions led by Jefferson Davis, Richard Johnson, and Little Phil Sheridan, marched south along the Nolensville Turnpike before swinging to the east and marching toward Murfreesboro. Finally, George H. Thomas's center wing, which included divisions led by Lovell Rousseau, James Negley, Speed Fry and Robert Mitchell, moved via the Wilson Turnpike along the Nashville and Decatur Railroad before swinging eastward and using the same route of Crittenden's wing along the Nashville and Chattanooga Railroad.

Thomas

Rosecrans would prove time and again over the next year that fighting pitched battles was hardly his strong suit, but at least when he faced Bragg, his grand movements were typically successful. While separating his three wings left each one vulnerable if they could be attacked and defeated in detail, Bragg simply didn't have enough men to do the job, and by marching in three columns, Bragg had to pull back William Hardee's men toward Murfreesboro to avoid having them turned, and he resolved to stand his ground there, leading Hardee to later complain, "The field of battle offered no particular advantages for defense."

Despite the fact Murfreesboro was only about 20 miles away from Nashville, Rosecrans's army did not reach the outskirts until December 29, a whole 3 days of marching, thanks in part to Wheeler's cavalry and the commander's caution. And despite that caution or perhaps because of it, Confederate cavalry had their way with the Union army before the battle, and Wheeler captured 1,000 prisoners and burned supplies riding completely around the Army of the Cumberland.

Wheeler

Meanwhile, the left wing of Rosecrans's army nearly suffered a disaster on December 29 due to the mistaken belief that they could occupy Murfreesboro itself. In addition to being a Confederate hotbed, General Crittenden failed to realize that the Confederate army had been firmly camped there for nearly a month. Rosecrans reported what happened that afternoon:

"About 3 p.m. a signal message coming from the front, from General Palmer, that he was in sight of Murfreesborough, and that the enemy were running, an order was sent to General Crittenden to send a division to occupy Murfreesborough. This led General Crittenden, on reaching the enemy's front, to order Harker's brigade to cross the river at a ford on his left, where he surprised a regiment of Breckinridge's division and drove it back on its main line, not more than 500 yards distant, in considerable confusion; and he held this position until General Crittenden was advised, by prisoners captured by Harker's brigade, that Breckinridge was in force on his front, when, it being dark, he ordered the brigade back across the river, and reported the circumstances to the commanding general on his arrival, to whom he apologized for not having carried out the order to occupy Murfreesborough. The general approved of his action, of course, the order to occupy Murfreesborough having been based on the information received from General Crittenden's advance division that the enemy were retreating from Murfreesborough."

On Monday, December 29, Rosecrans began forming his battle line north and west of Stones River, leading Bragg to believe that Rosecrans was going to try to turn his left flank. As a result,

Bragg pulled one of Hardee's divisions from his right flank and marched them to the left flank, . Bragg explained:

"Late on Monday it became apparent the enemy was extending his right, so as to flank us on the left. McCown's division, in reserve, was promptly thrown to that flank and added to the command of Lieutenant-General Polk. The enemy not meeting our expectations of making an attack on Tuesday, which was consumed in artillery firing and heavy skirmishing, with the exception of a dash late in the evening on the left of Withers' division, which was repulsed and severely punished, it was determined to assail him on Wednesday morning, the 31st. For this purpose, Cleburne's division, Hardee's corps, was moved from the second line on the right to the corresponding position on the left, and Lieuten-ant-General Hardee was ordered to that point and assigned to the command of that and McCown's division. This disposition, the result of necessity, left me no reserve, but Breckinridge's command on the right, now not threatened, was regarded as a source of supply for any re enforcements absolutely necessary to other parts of the field. Stone's River, at its then stage, was fordable at almost any point for infantry, and at short intervals perfectly practicable for artillery.

These dispositions completed, Lieutenant-General Hardee was ordered to assail the enemy at daylight on Wednesday, the 31st, the attack to be taken up by Lieutenant-General Polk's command in succession to the right flank, the move to be made by a constant wheel to the right, on Polk's right flank as a pivot, the object being to force the enemy back on Stone's River, and, if practicable, by the aid of the cavalry, cut him off from his base of operations and supplies by the Nashville pike. The lines were now bivouacked at a distance in places of not more than 500 yards, the camp-fires of the two being within distinct view. Wharton's cavalry brigade had been held on our left to watch and check the movements of the enemy in that direction, and to prevent his cavalry from gaining the railroad in our rear, the preservation of which was of vital importance. In this he was aided by Brig. Gen. A. Buford, who had a small command of about 600 new cavalry. The duty was most ably, gallantly, and successfully performed."

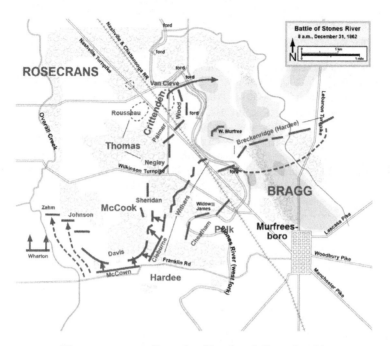

The movements on December 30 and early December 31

As Bragg was planning to use the men on his left flank to attack the Union's right flank in the morning of the 31st, Rosecrans was planning to use Crittenden's left wing to attack the Confederates' right flank around the same time:

"A meeting of the corps commanders was called at the headquarters of the commanding general for this evening. General Thomas arrived early, received his instructions, and retired. General Crittenden, with whom the commanding general had talked freely during the afternoon, was sent for, but was excused at the request of his chief of staff, who sent word that he was very much fatigued and was asleep. Generals McCook and Stanley arrived about 9 o'clock, to whom was explained the following plan of battle.

McCook was to occupy the most advantageous position, refusing his right as much as practicable and necessary to secure it, to receive the attack of the enemy; or, if that did not come, to attack himself, sufficient to hold all the force on his front; Thomas and Palmer to open with skirmishing, and engage the enemy's center and left as far as the river; Crittenden to cross Van Cleve's division at the lower ford, covered and supported by the sappers and miners, and to advance on Breckinridge; Wood's division to follow by brigades, crossing at the upper ford and moving on Van Cleve's right, to carry everything before them into Murfreesborough. This would have given us two divisions against one, and, as soon as Breckinridge had been dislodged from his position, the batteries of Wood's division, taking position on the heights east of Stone's River, in advance, would see the enemy's works in reverse, would dislodge them, and enable Palmer's division to press them back, and drive them westward across the river or through the woods, while Thomas, sustaining the movement on the center, would advance on the right of Palmer, crushing their right, and Crittenden's corps, advancing, would take Murfreesborough, and then, moving westward on the Franklin road, get in their flank and rear and drive them into the country toward Salem, with the prospect of cutting off their retreat and probably destroying their army.

It was explained to them that this combination, insuring us a vast superiority on our left, required for its success that General McCook should be able to hold his position for three hours; that, if necessary to recede at all, he should recede, as he had advanced on the preceding day, slowly and steadily, refusing his right, thereby rendering our success certain.

Having thus explained the plan, the general commanding addressed General McCook as follows: "You know the ground; you have fought over it; you know its difficulties. Can you hold your present position for three hours? To which General McCook responded, "Yes, I think I can." The general commanding then said, 6, I don't like the facing so much to the east, but must confide that to you, who know the ground. If you don't think your present the best position, change it. It is only necessary for you to make things sure." And the officers then returned to their commands.

At daylight on the morning of the 31st the troops breakfasted and stood to their arms, and by 7 o'clock were preparing for the battle."

Essentially, both armies were attacking with their left and hoping their right could hold on long enough for their own attack to have time to work. Both sides were confident, and Phil Sheridan later noted in his memoirs, "The precision that had characterized every manoeuvre of the past three days, and the exactness with which each corps and division fell into its allotted place on the evening of the 30th, indicated that at the outset of the campaign a well-digested plan of operations had been prepared for us; and although the scheme of the expected battle was not known to subordinates of my grade, yet all the movements up to this time had been so successfully and accurately made as to give much promise for the morrow, and when night fell there was general anticipation of the best results to the Union army."

Little Phil Sheridan

The night before the battle began in earnest, the two sides were bivouacked so close to each other that the armies' respective bands played music to each other across the battlefield, with the Union bands playing Yankee Doodle and dueling it out with Confederate renditions of Dixie and the Bonnie Blue Flag. When one of the bands switched to Home Sweet Home, other bands started playing the song, and men on both sides sang together.

Unfortunately for them, the harmonies of that night would be replaced by the thunderous volleys of artillery and musketry a few hours later.

Chapter 3: December 31

Rosecrans's report suggests that McCook was anticipating an attack on the Union right and would attempt to hold out for 3 hours, but Sheridan noted that his wing commander McCook seemed overly optimistic despite reports of Confederate movements in the early morning of the 31st:

"At 2 o'clock on the morning of the 31st General Sill came back to me to report that on his front a continuous movement of infantry and artillery had been going on all night within the Confederate lines, and that he was convinced that Bragg was massing on our right with the purpose of making an attack from that direction early in the morning. After discussing for a few minutes the probabilities of such a course on the part of the enemy, I thought McCook should be made acquainted with what was going on, so Sill and I went back to see him at his headquarters, not far from the Griscom House, where we found him sleeping on some straw in the angle of a worm-fence. I waked him up and communicated the intelligence, and our consequent impressions. He talked the matter over with us for some little time, but in view of the offensive-defensive part he was to play in the coming battle, did not seem to think that there was a necessity for any further dispositions than had already been taken. He said that he thought Johnson's division would be able to take care of the right, and seemed confident that the early assault which was to be made from Rosecrans's left would anticipate and check the designs which we presaged."

Action on the morning of December 31

One problem with Rosecrans's plan and McCook's optimism was that Bragg's army was ready to attack before Crittenden's wing crossed the Stones River on the other side of the field to attack the Confederates' right flank, but perhaps the most inexplicable problem was that some of McCook's men were not ready to defend when one of Hardee's divisions led by John McCown began the attack at dawn. Despite Sheridan's report to McCook, and Rosecrans's battle plan being discussed the night before, for some reason the Union soldiers in Richard Johnson's division were caught completely by surprise while eating breakfast when the Confederates struck.

Not surprisingly, Johnson's division was routed and sent into a panicked retreat, with the Confederates in dogged pursuit. As McCown and Hardee lost control of the pursuing Confederates, they began drifting to the left, creating a gap in the Confederate line that was then filled by Patrick Cleburne's division on their right. Cleburne, known as the "Stonewall Jackson of the West", was perhaps the most able division commander in the West, and his men began sweeping away the Union defenders on their right. The Confederates ran right past the campfires that were cooking Union soldiers' breakfasts and started capturing Union artillery batteries before they had even fired off a round. Johnson's division suffered over 50% casualties, a number of them simply being captured.

Bragg reported the effects of McCown's attack and the problem that developed as a result of the Confederates' pursuit of the fleeing Federals:

"The failure of Major-General McCown to execute during the night an order for a slight change in the line of his division, and which had to be done the next morning, caused some delay in the general and vigorous assault by Lieutenant-General Hardee. But about 7 o'clock the rattle of musketry and roar of artillery announced the beginning of the conflict. The enemy was taken completely by surprise. General and staff officers were not mounted, artillery horses not hitched, and infantry not formed. A hot and inviting breakfast of coffee and other luxuries, to which our gallant and hardy men had long been strangers, was found upon the fire unserved, and was left while we pushed on to the enjoyment of a more inviting feast, that of captured artillery, fleeing battalions, and hosts of craven prisoners begging for the lives they had forfeited by their acts of brutality and atrocity.

While thus routing and pushing the enemy in his front, Lieutenant-General [W. J.] Hardee announced to me by a messenger that the movement was not being as promptly executed by Major-General Cheatham's command on his right (the left of Lieutenant-General Polk's corps) as he expected, and that his line was, consequently, exposed to an enfilade fire from the enemy's artillery in that front."

As Johnson's division disintegrated, Jefferson Davis's division tried to quickly put up a defense, only to be routed by Cleburne's attack quickly. David would later report:

"The night passed off quietly until about daylight, when the enemy's forces were observed by our pickets to be in motion. Their object could not, however, with certainty, be determined until near sunrise, when a vigorous attack was made upon

Willich's and Kirk's brigades. These troops seemed not to have been fully prepared for the assault, and, with little or no resistance, retreated from their position, leaving their artillery in the hands of the enemy. This left my right brigade exposed to a flank movement, which the enemy was now rapidly executing, and compelled me to order Post's brigade to fall back and partially change its front. Simultaneous with this movement the enemy commenced a heavy and very determined attack on both Carlin's and Woodruff's brigades. These brigades were fully prepared for the attack, and received it with veteran courage. The conflict was fierce in the extreme on both sides. Our loss was heavy and that of the enemy no less. It was, according to my observations, the best contested point of the day, and would have been held, but for the overwhelming force moving so persistently against my right. Carlin, finding his right flank being so severely pressed, and threatened with being turned, ordered his troops to retire."

Despite the fact that two entire Union divisions on the right had quickly left the line, news of just how bad the situation was on the Union right was not initially reported to Rosecrans, who explained, "Within an hour from the time of the opening of the battle, a staff officer from General McCook arrived, announcing to me that the right wing was heavily pressed and needed assistance; but I was not advised of the rout of Willich's and Kirk's brigades, nor of the rapid withdrawal of Davis' division, necessitated thereby--moreover, having supposed his wing posted more compactly, and his right more refused than it really was, the direction of the noise of battle did not indicate to me the true state of affairs. I consequently directed him to return and direct General McCook to dispose his troops to the best advantage, and to hold his ground obstinately. Soon after, a second officer from General McCook arrived, and stated that the right wing was being driven--a fact that was but too manifest by the rapid movement of the noise of battle toward the north."

Once it became clearer that the right wing was facing disaster, Rosecrans pulled back Crittenden's wing and aborted that attack so that he could start shifting men to shore up his right flank. It would take Johnson nearly three hours to rally his broken division several miles in the rear, leaving others to try to deal with the emergency. At one point, Rosecrans was in the thick of shuffling his line around when his chief of staff, Col. Julius Garesché, was beheaded by a cannonball right next to him and covered him in Garesché's blood. Rosecrans explained how he reformed his line:

"General Thomas was immediately dispatched to order Rousseau, then in reserve, into the cedar brakes to the right and rear of Sheridan. General Crittenden was ordered to suspend Van Cleve's movement across the river, on the left, and to cover the crossing with one brigade, and move the other two brigades westward across the fields toward the railroad for a reserve. Wood was also directed to suspend his preparations for crossing, and to hold Hascall in reserve. At this moment fugitives and stragglers from

McCook's corps began to make their appearance through the cedar-brakes in such numbers that I became satisfied that McCook's corps was routed. I, therefore, directed General Crittenden to send Van Cleve in to the right of Rousseau; Wood to send Colonel Harker's brigade farther down the Murfreesborough pike, to go in and attack the enemy on the right of Van Cleve's, the Pioneer Brigade meanwhile occupying the knoll of ground west of Murfreesborough pike, and about 400 or 500 yards in rear of Palmer's center, supporting Stokes' battery (see accompanying drawing). Sheridan, after sustaining four successive attacks, gradually swung his right from a southeasterly to a northwesterly direction, repulsing the enemy four times, losing the gallant General Sill, of his right, and Colonel Roberts, of his left brigade, when, having exhausted his ammunition, Negley's division being in the same predicament, and heavily pressed, after desperate fighting, they fell back from the position held at the commencement, through the cedar woods, in which Rousseau's division, with a portion of Negley's and Sheridan's, met the advancing enemy and checked his movements."

As men from Thomas's center began shifting to the Union right, Sheridan was taking extreme measures to protect his own division's flank, which he explained in his memoirs:

"Both Johnson's and Davis's divisions were now practically gone from our line, having retired with a loss of all formation, and they were being closely pursued by the enemy, whose columns were following the arc of a circle that would ultimately carry him in on my rear. In consequence of the fact that this state of things would soon subject me to a fire in reverse, I hastily withdrew Sill's brigade and the reserve regiments supporting it, and ordered Roberts's brigade, which at the close of the enemy's second repulse had changed front toward the south and formed in column of regiments, to cover the withdrawal by a charge on the Confederates as they came into the timber where my right had originally rested. Roberts made the charge at the proper time, and was successful in checking the enemy's advance, thus giving us a breathingspell, during which I was able to take up a new position with Schaefer's and Sill's brigades on the commanding ground to the rear, where Hescock's and Houghtaling's batteries had been posted all the morning.

The general course of this new position was at right angles with my original line, and it took the shape of an obtuse angle, with my three batteries at the apex. Davis, and Carlin of his division, endeavored to rally their men here on my right, but their efforts were practically unavailing, though the calm and cool appearance of Carlin, who at the time was smoking a stumpy pipe, had some effect, and was in strong contrast to the excited manner of Davis, who seemed overpowered by the disaster that had befallen his command. But few could be rallied, however, as the men were badly demoralized, and most of them fell back beyond the Wilkinson pike, where they reorganized behind the troops of General Thomas."

The initial Confederate attack had been so successful that it was actually making it all but impossible for Bragg to make a coordinated push with both Hardee's men and Polk's men immediately on their right. As previously noted, there was a delay in an attack by Benjamin Cheatham's division, and when Cheatham's division and Jones Withers's division made their concerted attack in the late morning, it was more of a second assault than anything else. Withers was repulsed by Sheridan's heavily pressed division, while Cheatham's assault was made piecemeal in such a haphazard way that he was later accused of being drunk. Even still, Sheridan's brigadiers were all mortally wounded on the field, and his division lost nearly a third of its men in just a few hours. Before noon, Sheridan's division was so depleted and short on ammunition that he had to pull it out of the line and reform behind George H. Thomas's reinforcements. Sheridan explained:

"As the enemy was recoiling from his first attack, I received a message from Rosecrans telling me that he was making new dispositions, and directing me to hold on where I was until they were completed. From this I judged that the existing conditions of the battle would probably require a sacrifice of my command, so I informed Roberts and Schaefer that we must be prepared to meet the demand on us by withstanding the assault of the enemy, no matter what the outcome. Every energy was therefore bent to the simple holding of our ground, and as ammunition was getting scarce, instructions were given throughout the command to have it reserve its fire till the most effective moment. In a little while came a second and a third assault, and although they were as daring and furious as the first, yet in each case the Confederates were repulsed, driven back in confusion, but not without deadly loss to us, for the noble Roberts was killed, and Colonel Harrington, of the Twenty-Seventh Illinois, who succeeded to his brigade, was mortally wounded a few minutes later. I had now on the death-roll three brigade commanders, and the loss of subordinate officers and men was appalling, but their sacrifice had accomplished the desired result; they had not fallen in vain. Indeed, the bravery and tenacity of my division gave to Rosecrans the time required to make new dispositions, and exacted from our foes the highest commendations."

By 10:00 a.m., Rosecrans's army was holding on for dear life. Nearly 30 guns and 3,000 Union soldiers had been captured, and the right flank was a complete mess. Their saving grace was the topography; Crittenden's left wing was behind the Stones River while the Confederates opposite them were on the eastern side across the river, making it more difficult to attack that side and start pressing both Union flanks simultaneously. As a result, when the Union's defensive line was being driven back, it was being driven back into a tighter line, shaped like a U, making it that much easier to reinforce their own lines even as the Confederate line began to spread further and further apart. As Bragg's biographer Grady McWhiny explained, "Unless the Union army collapsed at the first onslaught, it would be pushed back into a tighter and stronger defensive position as the battle continued, while the Confederate forces would gradually lose momentum, become disorganized, and grow weaker. Like a snowball, the Federals would pick up strength from the debris of battle if they retreated in good order. But the Confederates would inevitably unwind like a ball of string as they advanced."

Any hopes Bragg had of driving the Union's left flank were undone by John Breckinridge, whose division of Hardee's corps was on the far right. Breckinridge had been one of the Democratic presidential candidates along with "The Little Giant" Stephen Douglas in 1860, and both of them lost to Lincoln that November, but his political importance had all but assured he would receive an important military command at the outbreak of the war. Unfortunately for both the North and South, political generals were typically inept, and that was definitely the case with Breckinridge. Breckinridge was too slow to notice Crittenden's attack had been aborted, so he refused to send some of his brigades to the Confederate left to reinforce the attack and also refused to move forward himself. Making matters worse, Bragg received bad intelligence about Union movements that made him believe a new threat to his right flank was imminent. Not only did Bragg countermand the orders for Breckinridge to send two brigades, he also began reinforcing Breckinridge's flank:

"As early as 10 a.m. Major-General Breckinridge was called on for one brigade, and soon after for a second, to re-enforce, or act as a reserve to, Lieutenant-General Hardee.

His reply to the first call represented the enemy crossing Stone's River in heavy force in his immediate front, and on receiving the second order he informed me they had already crossed in heavy force and were advancing on him in two lines. He was immediately ordered not to await attack, but to advance and meet them. About this same time a report reached me that a heavy force of the enemy's infantry was advancing on the Lebanon road, about 5 miles in Breckinridge's front. Brigadier-General Pegram, who had been sent to that road to cover the flank of the infantry with his cavalry brigade (save two regiments detached with Wheeler and Wharton), was ordered forward immediately to develop any such movement. The orders for the two brigades from Breckinridge were countermanded, while dispositions were made, at his request, to re-enforce him."

In essence, while the Confederates on the left were in a dogfight trying to break the Union's right flank, Bragg began mistakenly bolstering his own right despite the fact there were no major Union forces in Breckinridge's front. It was not until 11:00 a.m. that Breckinridge actually moved some of his men forward only to find nothing in his front; Bragg would later accuse him of drunkenness.

Breckinridge

Breckinridge dithered so much that it would not be until the middle of the afternoon that his men were used in an assault, and as fate would have it they would be part of the most famous fighting of the entire battle. As the Federals kept reinforcing and defending the western side of the Nashville Turnpike, Confederates from Breckinridge's division and Leonidas Polk's corps began advancing and smashed into the center and left of the Union line, where it was sharply repulsed by Col. William B. Hazen's brigade in a rocky wooded area that would become known as "Hell's Half-Acre". With Sheridan having been forced to form his division at a right angle, Hazen's brigade had become the salient in the U-shaped line, and if it was routed, the Confederates would have split the Army of the Cumberland in two, separating Crittenden from McCook and George H. Thomas, and would have been in the rear of both isolated parts of the Union army. Hazen and his regimental commanders barely held on in the small 4 acre part of their line, determined to stand "even if it cost the last man we had." Hazen would be wounded in the shoulder but almost immediately be promoted for gallantry that day, and veterans of his brigade would actually erect a monument on the spot while the Civil War was still ongoing, making it the oldest Civil War monument.

Hazen

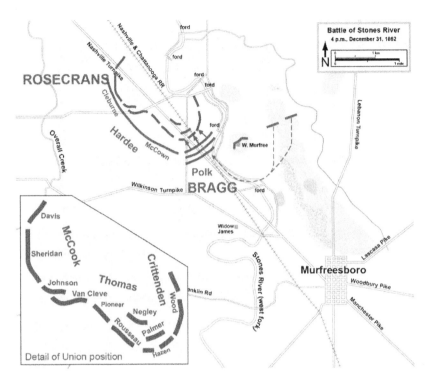

The Confederate assault in the afternoon

When Breckinridge's piecemeal attacks were repulsed by Hazen's brigade, and a second concerted attack with Polk's men were repulsed, the fighting had all but finished for the day. Polk's post-battle report detailed some of the confusion in the Confederate command that afternoon resulting from Breckinridge's delay:

My last reserve having been exhausted, the brigades of Major-General Breckinridge's division, and a small brigade of [Brigadier-]General J. K. Jackson, posted to guard our right flank, were the only troops left that had not been engaged. Four of these were ordered to report to me. They came in detachments of two brigades each, the first arriving nearly two hours after Donelson's attack, the other about an hour after the first. The commanders of these detachments, the first composed of the brigades of Generals [D. W.] Adams and Jackson, the second under General Breckinridge in person, consisting of the brigades of General [William] Preston and Colonel [J. B.] Palmer, had pointed out to them the particular object to be accomplished, to wit, to drive in the enemy's left, and, especially, to dislodge him from his position in the Round Forest. Unfortunately, the opportune moment for putting in these detachments had passed. Could they have been thrown upon the enemy's left immediately following Chalmers' and Donelson's assault in quick succession, the extraordinary strength of his position would have availed him nothing. That point would have been carried, and his left, driven back on his panic-stricken right, would have completed his confusion and insured an utter rout. It was, however, otherwise, and the time lost between Donelson's attack and the coming up of these detachments in succession enabled the enemy to recover his self-possession, to mass a number of heavy batteries, and concentrate a strong infantry force on the positions, and thus make a successful attack very difficult. Nevertheless, the brigades of Adams and Jackson assailed the enemy's line with energy, and, after a severe contest, were compelled to yield and fall back. They were promptly rallied by General Breckinridge, who, having preceded his other brigades, reached the ground at that moment, but as they were very much cut up, they were not required to renew the attack. The brigades of Preston and Palmer, on arriving, renewed the assault with the same undaunted determination, but as another battery had been added since the previous attack, to a position already strong and difficult of access, this assault was alike ineffectual. The enemy, though not driven from his position, was severely punished, and, as the day was far spent, it was not deemed advisable to renew the attack that evening, and the troops held the line they occupied for the night."

That night, Rosecrans and his senior officers had to decide whether to retreat or stay and fight more. Rosecrans was pressed by some to retreat, but he was determined to stay and fight, and he was supported by George H. Thomas, who famously stated at the council of war, "This army does not retreat." Rosecrans would later write of December 31:

"We had lost heavily in killed and wounded, and a considerable number in stragglers and prisoners; also twenty-eight pieces of artillery, the horses having been slain, and our troops being unable to with draw them by hand over the rough ground; but the enemy had been thoroughly handled and badly damaged at all points, having had no success where we had open ground and our troops were properly posted: none which did not depend on the original crushing in of our right and the superior masses which were in consequence brought to bear upon the narrow front of Sheridan's and Negley's divisions, and a part of Palmer's, coupled with the scarcity of ammunition, caused by the circuitous road which the train had taken, and the inconvenience of getting it from a remote distance through the cedars. Orders were given for the issue of all the spare ammunition, and we found that we had enough for another battle, the only question being where that battle was to be fought.

It was decided, in order to complete our present lines, that the left should be retired some 250 yards to a more advantageous ground, the extreme left resting on Stone's

River, above the lower ford, and extending to Stokes' battery. Starkweather's and Walker's brigades arriving near the close of the evening, the former bivouacked in close column, in reserve, in rear of McCook's left, and the latter was posted on the left of Sheridan, near the Murfreesborough pike, and next morning relieved Van Cleve, who returned to his position in the left wing."

Rosecrans didn't believe his army was defeated, but Bragg certainly did, sending a telegram to Richmond that night claiming, "The enemy has yielded his strong position and is falling back. We occupy whole field and shall follow him...God has granted us a happy New Year."

Chapter 4: January 1-3

Bragg may have believed Rosecrans was defeated, but he had also lost 9,000 men himself on December 31, a staggering 25% of his men, and he had failed to deliver the finishing stroke. Both armies mostly decided to lick their wounds on New Year's Day, with Bragg only sending forth a couple of reconnaissances-in-force to ascertain whether Rosecrans was reorganizing his line, or, as Bragg figured, preparing to retreat:

"At dawn on Thursday morning, January 1, orders were sent to the several commanders to press forward their skirmishers, feel the enemy, and report any change in his position. Major-General Breckinridge had been transferred to the right of Stone's River, to resume the command of that position, now held by two of his brigades. It was soon reported that no change had occurred, except the withdrawal of the enemy from the advanced position occupied by his left flank. Finding, upon further examination, that this was the case, the right flank of Lieutenant-General Polk's corps was thrown forward to occupy the ground for which we had so obstinately contended the evening before. This shortened our line considerably, and gave us possession of the entire battle-field, from which we gleaned the spoils and trophies throughout the day and transferred them rapidly to the rear. A careful reconnaissance of the enemy's position was ordered, and the most of the cavalry was put in motion for the roads in his rear, to cut off his trains and develop any movement. It was soon ascertained that he was still in very heavy force all along our front, occupying a position strong by nature and improved by such work as could be done at night and by his reserves. In a short time reports from the cavalry informed me heavy trains were moving toward Nashville, some of the wagons loaded and all the ambulances filled with wounded. These were attacked at different places; many wagons were destroyed and hundreds of prisoners paroled. No doubt this induced the enemy to send large escorts of artillery, infantry, and cavalry with later trains, and thus the impression was made on our ablest cavalry commanders that a retrograde movement was going on. Our forces, greatly wearied and much reduced by heavy losses, were held ready to avail themselves of any change in the enemy's position, but it was deemed unadvisable to assail him as then established. The whole day, after these dispositions, was passed without an important movement on either side, and was consumed by us in gleaning the battlefield, burying the dead, and replenishing ammunition."

As Bragg was laboring under the impression that Rosecrans was retreating, Rosecrans was actually going about trying to bolster his defensive line. To do so, he ordered Van Cleve's division from Crittenden's wing to cross the Stones River and take the high ground, allowing him to post batteries there. Although this meant that Rosecrans was effectively splitting his army, with Crittenden's wing on the east side of the Stones River and Thomas and McCook on the west, the river itself would cover the gap, and the Union soldiers still controlled the road that would allow their wings to link back together.

On the morning of January 2, Bragg was still anticipating a Union retreat, but now he put together plans to assault the Army of the Cumberland, using Breckinridge's men on their right flank:

"At daylight on Friday, the 2d, the orders to feel the enemy and ascertain his position were repeated with the same results. The cavalry brigades of Wheeler and Wharton had returned during the night greatly exhausted from long-continued service with but little rest or food to either men or horses. Both commanders reported the indications from the enemy's movements the same. Allowing them only a few hours to feed and rest, and sending the two detached regiments back to Pegram's brigade, Wharton was ordered to the right flank across Stone's River, to assume command in that quarter and keep me advised of any change. Wheeler with his brigade was ordered to gain the enemy's rear again, and remain until he could definitely report whether any retrograde movement was being made. Before Wharton had taken his position, observation excited my suspicions in regard to a movement having been made by the enemy across Stone's River immediately in Breckinridge's front. Reconnaissances by several staff officers soon developed the fact that a division had quietly crossed unopposed and established themselves on and under cover of an eminence, marked B on map No. 2, from which Lieutenant-General Polk's line was both commanded and enfiladed. The dislodgment of this force or the withdrawal of Polk's line was an evident necessity. The latter involved consequences not to be entertained. Orders were accordingly given for the concentration of the whole of Major-General Breckinridge's division in front of the position to be taken, the addition to his command of ten 12-pounder Napoleon guns, under Capt. F. H. Robertson, an able and accomplished artillery officer, and for the cavalry forces of Wharton and Pegram, about 2,000 men, to join in the attack on his right. Major-General Breckinridge was sent for and advised of the movement and its objects, the securing and holding of the position which protected Polk's flank and gave us command of the enemy's by which to enfilade him. He was informed of the forces placed at his disposal, and instructed with them to drive the enemy back, crown the his, intrench his artillery, and hold the position.

To distract their attention from our real object, a heavy artillery fire was ordered to be opened from Polk's front at the exact hour at which the' movement was to begin. At other points throughout both lines all was quiet. General Breckinridge at 3.30 p.m. reported he would advance at 4 o'clock."

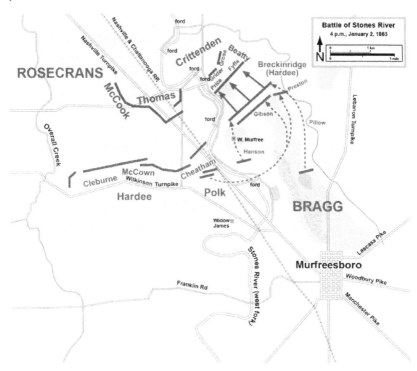

The beginning of the attack

It's unclear why Bragg would rely on Breckinridge to make a massive attack after his performance on December 31, and on top of that Breckinridge thought the attack was suicidal, given that the Union defenders had all of the previous day to fortify their spot and post their artillery. Despite initial protestations, Breckinridge's men pushed forward as ordered and were able to steadily advance, but it only had the effect of pushing the Union defenders across McFadden Ford and safely into the rest of the Union defensive line held by Thomas and McCook. While Breckinridge's men kept moving forward, they were met by artillery fire from batteries safely posted across the Stones River.

The Confederate attack stalled around McFadden Ford, suffering enfilading battery fire that helped inflict nearly 2,000 casualties in the first hour, but Bragg still intended to try to press the attack, as he explained in his report:

"Polk's batteries promptly opened fire and were soon answered by the enemy. A heavy cannonade of some fifteen minutes was succeeded by the fire of musketry, which soon became general. The contest was short and severe; the enemy was driven back and the eminence gained, but the movement as a whole was a failure, and the position was again yielded. Our forces were moved, unfortunately, so far to the left as to throw a portion of them into and over Stone's River, where they encountered heavy masses of the enemy, while those against whom they were intended to operate on our side of the river had a destructive enfilade on our whole line. Our second line was so close to the front as to receive the enemy's fire, and, returning it, took their friends in rear. The cavalry force was left entirely out of the action. Learning from my own staff officers, sent to the scene, of the disorderly retreat being made by General Breckinridge's division, Brigadier-General Patton Anderson's fine brigade of Mississippians (the nearest body of troops) was promptly ordered to his relief."

Bragg was so ignorant of the situation in that sector that while he was trying to reinforce Breckinridge's men, Negley's division of Thomas's wing began its own counterattack, pushing Breckinridge's division into full retreat. Breckinridge was so shaken by the repulse of his attack that he rode around part of his line, comprised of a brigade of Kentucky troops known as the Orphan Brigade due to the fact Kentucky was occupied by Union armies, and cried out, "My poor Orphans! My poor Orphans!"

By the time Breckinridge's attack was finished, night was falling, and Bragg went about reorganizing Breckinridge's division and reforming his line. By the beginning of January 3, both armies were virtually in the same lines as the last few days.

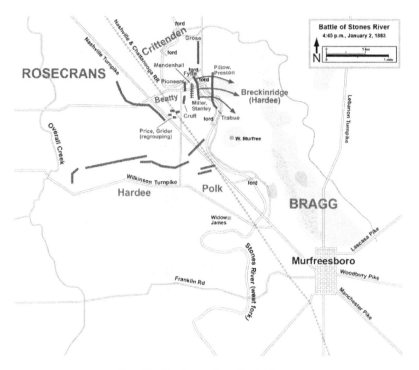

Breckinridge's attack stalls. 4:45 p.m.

On January 1, Bragg woke up certain of victory and confident that Rosecrans would retreat. On January 3, Bragg woke up certain that he had to retreat himself:

On Saturday morning, the 3d, our forces had been in line of battle for five days and nights, with but little rest, having no reserves; their baggage and tents had been loaded and the wagons were 4 miles off; their provisions, if cooked at all, were most imperfectly prepared, with scanty means; the weather had been severe from cold and almost constant rain, and we had no change of clothing, and in many places could not have fires. The necessary consequence was great exhaustion of officers and men, many having to be sent to the hospitals in the rear, and more still were beginning to straggle from their commands, an evil from which we had so far suffered but little. During the whole of this day the rain continued to fall with little intermission, and the rapid rise in Stone's River indicated it would soon be unfordable. Late on Friday night I had received the captured papers of Major-General [A. McD.] McCook, commanding one corps d'armée of the enemy, showing their effective strength to have been very near, if not quite, 70,000 men. Before noon, reports from Brigadier-General Wheeler satisfied me the enemy, instead of retiring, was receiving re-enforcements. Common prudence and the safety of my army, upon which even the safety of our cause depended, left no doubt on my mind as to the necessity of my withdrawal from so unequal a contest. My orders were accordingly given about noon for the movement of the trains, and for the necessary preparation of the troops.

Chapter 5: The Aftermath of the Battle of Stones River

"Just as at Perryville, Bragg seemed to change under stress from a bold and aggressive attacker to a hesitant and cautious retreater. He had, of course, sound reasons for withdrawing from Murfreesboro. His principal subordinates advised him to retreat. He had lost nearly 30% of his men in the recent battles; if forced to fight again without some rest, his army might disintegrate. But his decision to retreat allowed his enemies to charge that once again Bragg had lost his nerve." – Grady McWhiny

Rosecrans would barely give chase as Bragg retreated, in part because it was raining heavily on January 3, making the use of artillery impossible. By the following day, Rosecrans learned that Bragg had retreated. Like Bragg, who claimed it was necessary to retreat due to his army being outnumbered, Rosecrans incorrectly claimed in his report to Washington that his men had defeated a superior army, writing, "On the whole, it is evident that we fought superior numbers on unknown ground; inflicted much more injury than we suffered; were always superior on equal ground with equal numbers, and failed of a most crushing victory on Wednesday by the extension and direction of our right wing."

On January 5, the Union army occupied Murfreesboro, and Rosecrans was all too happy to stop there, confident that he had just scored an important campaign victory. While it's true that Rosecrans held possession of the field after the battle and occupied Murfreesboro, the fighting itself was a total stalemate, and almost a disaster for the Army of the Cumberland. All told, there were nearly 25,000 casualties in the battle, most on December 31, with a total of nearly 13,000 Federals and 12,000 Confederates killed, wounded or captured. It was the costliest battle of the Civil War to date and the 6th costliest battle of the entire war.

Sheridan described the ghastly scene on the battlefield after the fighting was done:

"As soon as possible after the Confederate retreat I went over the battle-field to collect such of my wounded as had not been carried off to the South and to bury my dead. In the cedars and on the ground where I had been so fiercely assaulted when the battle opened on the morning of the 31st, evidences of the bloody struggle appeared on every hand in the form of broken fire-arms, fragments of accoutrements, and splintered trees. The dead had nearly all been left unburied, but as there was likelihood of their mutilation by roving swine, the bodies had mostly been collected in piles at different points and inclosed by rail fences. The sad duties of interment and of caring for the wounded were completed by the 5th.”

Rosecrans's belief that he had scored a big victory was echoed by the Lincoln Administration, which was only too happy to credit him and call the battle a victory after the debacle at Fredericksburg less than three weeks earlier. But while it certainly succeeded in permanently stopping Bragg from threatening Kentucky, Rosecrans has been criticized for his management of the battle by some historians, particularly for his handling of the dispositions on the night of the 30th. Henry M. Cist, a member of Rosecrans's staff, wrote in his history *The Army Of The Cumberland*:

“Why did Rosecrans's plan of battle miscarry so fatally and Bragg's come so near absolute success? The fault was not in the plan as conceived by the former. The near success of the latter proved a vindication of that. The originator of the plan was not at fault personally, for at no time during the battle did he falter or prove unequal to his command. When called on to give up his plan of the offensive and assume the defensive to save his army, the wonderful power of Rosecrans as a general over troops was never displayed to a greater advantage. With the blood from a slight wound on his check, in a light blue army overcoat, through the mud and rain of the battle-field, he rode along the line inspiring his troops with the confidence he felt as to the final result. To Rosecrans there was but one outcome to the battle at Stone's River, and that was victory. When some of his general officers advised retreat to Nashville, not for an instant did he falter in his determination to ‘fight or die right here.’ The demoralization of one of his division commanders was so great, that on Thursday afternoon, when the rebels were massing on Rosecrans's right, this general, commanding a division, announced to his brigade commanders that in the event of the anticipated assault resulting disastrously, he proposed to take his division and cut his way through to Nashville. To his troops--the greater part of whom had never seen Rosecrans under the enemy's fire--when on their return from the cedars, they formed anew in front of the Nashville pike--seeing the Commanding General of the army riding fearlessly on the extreme front, in the heat of battle, cool and collected, giving orders and encouraging his men--his mere presence was an inspiration. His personal bravery was never more fully shown than when he rode down to the ‘Round Forest’ with his staff, under fire, at the time Garesché was killed by a shell that only missed the chief by a few inches. In this ride Rosecrans had three mounted orderlies shot dead while following him. When the entire extent of McCook's disaster in its crushing force was revealed to him, he felt the full burden of his responsibility, and rising to the demands of the hour he was superb. Dashing from one point to another, quick to discern danger and ready to meet it, shrinking from no personal exposure, dispatching his staff on the gallop, hurrying troops into position, massing the artillery and forming his new lines on grounds of his own choosing, confident of ultimate success, and showing his troops that he had all confidence in them, it was worth months of an ordinary life-time to have been with Rosecrans when by his own unconquered spirit he plucked victory from defeat and glory from disaster.

But if the plan was not at fault, what was? Rosecrans started from Nashville for an offensive campaign, and before his plan of battle had met the test, he was compelled to abandon it, and assume the defensive. Where was the fault and who was to blame? The fault was McCook's defective line, and in part Rosecrans was responsible for it. He ought never to have trusted the formation of a line of battle so important to the safety of his whole army to McCook alone, and he certainly knew this. Rosecrans gave his personal attention to the left, but he should at least have ordered the change his quick eye detected as necessary in McCook's line, and not trusted to chance and McCook's ability to withstand the attack with his faulty line. No one who saw him at Stone's River the 31st of December will say aught against the personal bravery and courage of McCook under fire. All that he could do to aid in repairing the great disaster of that day he did to the best of his ability. He stayed with Davis's division under fire as long as it held together, and then gave personal directions to Sheridan's troops, in the gallant fight they made against overwhelming odds. As Rosecrans himself says in his official report of McCook, 'a tried, faithful, and loyal soldier, who bravely breasted the battle at Shiloh and Perryville, and as bravely on the bloody field of Stone's River.' But there is something more than mere physical bravery required in a general officer in command of as large a body of troops as a corps d'armee. As an instructor at West Point, McCook maintained a high rank. As a brigade and division commander under Buell, there was none his superior in the care and attention he gave his troops on the march, in camp, or on the drill-ground. His division at Shiloh as it marched to the front on the second day did him full credit, and in his handling of it on that field he did credit to it and to himself. What McCook lacked was the ability to handle large bodies of troops independently of a superior officer to give him commands. This was his experience at Perryville, and it was repeated at Stone's River. With the known results of Perryville, McCook ought never to have been placed in command of the 'right wing.' Rosecrans at Stone's River, of necessity was on the left, and being there he should have had a general in command of the right with greater military capacity than McCook. Rosecrans's confidence was so slight in his commander of the left that he felt his own presence was needed there in the movement of the troops in that part of the plan of battle.

Rosecrans in his report repeatedly speaks of 'the faulty line of McCook's formation on the right.' But he knew of this on the 30th, and told McCook that it was improperly placed. McCook did not think so. Rosecrans told him that it faced too much to the cast and not enough to the south, that it was too weak and long, and was liable to be flanked. Knowing all this and knowing McCook's pride of opinion, for McCook told him he 'did not see how he could make a better line,' or a 'better disposition of my troops,' it was the plain duty of Rosecrans to reform the line, to conform to what it should be in his judgment. The order to McCook to build camp fires for a mile beyond his right, was another factor that brought about the combination that broke the line on the right. Rosecrans was correct in the conception of this, in order to mislead Bragg and cause him to strengthen his left at the expense of his right. Had Bragg awaited Rosecrans's attack, this building of fires was correct--if it took troops away from the right to reinforce the left; but this it did not do. Bragg moved McCown and Cleburne's divisions from his right to his left on Tuesday, but after this Bragg brought none of his forces across the river until Wednesday afternoon. The building of the fires caused Bragg to prolong his lines, lengthening them to the extent that before Hardee struck Kirk's and Willich's brigades, he thought our line extended a division front to their right. Finding this not to be the case, he whirled his left with all the force of double numbers on to the right of McCook. The rebels then swinging around threw themselves in the rear of Johnson's division before they struck any troops on their front. Of course it is mere guess-work to say just what the outcome might have been of any other formation of the line, but it is safe to say that had the left instead of the centre of Hardee struck the right of McCook, there would have been a better chance for the troops on the extreme right of his line to have shown the spirit that was in them, before they were overpowered by mere superiority of numbers."

Perhaps the most surprising byproduct of the Battle of Stones River is that Rosecrans and Bragg would both be in position to command armies against each other the following year at the Battle of Chickamauga. Bragg's unsuccessful campaigns, culminating in the Battle of Perryville and the Battle of Stones River, led to harsh criticism from some of the men under his command, including the equally incompetent Lt. Gen. Leonidas Polk, as well as William Hardee and Simon Bolivar Buckner. Hardee would actually demand to be transferred out of Bragg's army before Chickamauga.

Bragg was a classmate of Jefferson Davis's at West Point, and it has long been asserted that Davis's friendship with Bragg kept the incompetent commander in a position too far above his station for too long. Bragg would not be relieved of command of the Army of Tennessee until nearly the end of 1863, by which time he had alienated most of his senior officers. General James Longstreet, who fought under Bragg at Chickamauga, later stated to Jefferson Davis, "Nothing but the hand of God can help as long as we have our present commander." General Joseph E. Johnston may have put it best when he quipped, "I know Mr. Davis thinks he can do a great many things other men would hesitate to attempt. For instance, he tried to do what God failed to do. He tried to make a soldier of Braxton Bragg."

Bragg would actually stay in command longer than Rosecrans, who was relieved after his disastrous performance at Chickamauga. Though he had been conspicuously gallant at the front during the near disaster at Stones River on December 31, he actually retreated from the field during the climactic fighting at Chickamauga and rode back to Chattanooga, where he was later allegedly found weeping and seeking solace from a staff priest. It would fall on his principal subordinate, George H. Thomas, to rally the remnants of the Army of the Cumberland at Chickamauga, make an impromptu defense, and save the army from potential destruction, all of which earned Thomas the famous nickname "The Rock of Chickamauga".

Rosecrans would be relieved soon after during the Confederate siege of Chattanooga, fittingly replaced in command of the Army of the Cumberland by George H. Thomas himself.

Bibliography

Connelly, Thomas L. Autumn of Glory: The Army of Tennessee 1862–1865. Baton Rouge: Louisiana State University Press, 1971.

Cozzens, Peter. No Better Place to Die: The Battle of Stones River. Urbana: University of Illinois Press, 1990.

Crittenden, Thomas L. "The Union Left at Stone's River." In Battles and Leaders of the Civil War, vol. 3, edited by Robert Underwood Johnson and Clarence C. Buel. New York: Century Co., 1884-1888.

Daniel, Larry J. Days of Glory: The Army of the Cumberland, 1861–1865. Baton Rouge: Louisiana State University Press, 2004.

Hess, Earl J. Banners to the Breeze: The Kentucky Campaign, Corinth, and Stones River. Lincoln: University of Nebraska Press, 2000.

Horn, Stanley F. The Army of Tennessee: A Military History. Indianapolis: Bobbs-Merrill, 1941.

McDonough, James Lee. "Battle of Stones River." In Battle Chronicles of the Civil War: 1862, edited by James M. McPherson. Connecticut: Grey Castle Press, 1989.

McWhiney, Grady. Braxton Bragg and Confederate Defeat. Vol. 1. New York: Columbia University Press, 1969 (additional material, Tuscaloosa: University of Alabama Press, 1991).

The Battle of Chickamauga

Chapter 1: The Summer of 1863

Of all the commanders who led armies during major battles of the Civil War, historians have by and large agreed that the most inept generals to face each other were the Union's William Rosecrans and the Confederacy's Braxton Bragg. The two generals' armies, the Union Army of the Cumberland and the Confederate Army of Tennessee, had already fought at the Battle of Stones River (Battle of Murfreesboro) at the end of 1862, inflicting massive casualties on each other without gaining an advantage.

During the first half of 1863, the two armies maneuvered around Chattanooga, Tennessee, one of the important railroad hubs of the theater. With Ulysses S. Grant laying siege to Vicksburg and trying to close off the Mississippi River, the Lincoln Administration hoped that a decisive campaign by Bragg in southern Tennessee would lay the groundwork for the capture of Atlanta, one of the Confederacy's most important cities.

That very thought terrorized the minds of Confederate officials and generals, even some of those fighting in the East. Early in 1863, Robert E. Lee's principal subordinate, James Longstreet, had advocated letting him take his corps west to try to relieve Vicksburg or conduct a campaign in Tennessee that would force Grant to stop his siege or send some of his men elsewhere. Lee had not wanted to detach any soldiers from his own army, given that it was badly outnumbered by the Union Army of the Potomac, but after the fall of Vicksburg and the defeat at Gettysburg, the situation had changed. Longstreet explained in his memoirs:

"To me the emergency seemed so grave that I decided to write the Honorable Secretary of War (excusing the informality under the privilege given in his request in May) expressing my opinion of affairs in that military zone. I said that the successful march of General Rosecrans's army through Georgia would virtually be the finishing stroke of the war; that in the fall of Vicksburg and the free flow of the Mississippi River the lungs of the Confederacy were lost; that the impending march would cut through the heart of the South, and leave but little time for the dissolution; that to my mind the remedy was to order the Army of Northern Virginia to defensive work, and send detachments to reinforce the army in Tennessee; to call detachments of other commands to the same service, and strike a crushing blow against General Rosecrans before he could receive reinforcing help; that our interior lines gave the opportunity, and it was only by the skilful use of them that we could reasonably hope to equalize our power to that of the better-equipped adversary; that the subject had not been mentioned to my commander, because like all others he was opposed to having important detachments of his army so far beyond his reach; that all must realize that our affairs were languishing, and that the only hope of reviving the waning cause was through the advantage of interior lines."

Longstreet

After the fall of Vicksburg, the Confederate high command had reached the same opinion, and during the end of July and into August they went about strengthening Bragg's Army of Tennessee. Bragg had about 50,000 men that summer, but Davis added the Department of East Tennessee, which included nearly 18,000 men under Maj. Gen. Simon B. Buckner, into Bragg's Department of Tennessee. Meanwhile, plans were set in motion to detach Longstreet's corps from Lee's Army of Northern Virginia and transfer it to Tennessee by rail.

As Bragg's army was being reinforced, there was another matter that Jefferson Davis had to work through: the internal squabbles among his generals. Bragg's previous campaigns (and their lack of successes) had led to harsh criticism from some of the men now nominally under his command, including the equally incompetent Lt. Gen. Leonidas Polk, as well as William Hardee and Simon Bolivar Buckner. In his official report to the Confederate government after the battle, Bragg hinted at how the mutual disdain among the senior officers in his department led to arguments over orders that summer:

"On August 20, it was ascertained certainly that the Federal army from Middle Tennessee, under General Rosecrans, had crossed the mountains to Stevenson and Bridgeport. His force of effective infantry and artillery amounted to fully 70,000, divided into four corps. About the same time General Burnside advanced from Kentucky toward Knoxville, East Tennessee, with a force estimated by the general commanding that department at over 25,000.

In view of the great superiority of numbers brought against him General Buckner concluded to evacuate Knoxville, and with a force of about 5,000 infantry and artillery and his cavalry took position in the vicinity of Loudon. Two brigades of his command (Frazer's, at Cumberland Gap, and Jackson's, in Northeast Tennessee) were thus severed from us.

The enemy having already obtained a lodgment in East Tennessee by another route, the continued occupation of Cumberland Gap became very hazardous to the garrison and comparatively unimportant to us. Its evacuation was accordingly ordered, but on the appeal of its commander, stating his resources and ability for defense, favorably indorsed by Major-General Buckner, the orders were suspended on August 31. The main body of our army was encamped near Chattanooga, while the cavalry force, much reduced and enfeebled by long service on short rations, was recruiting in the vicinity of Rome, Ga."

Hardee, in command of one of Bragg's corps, despised Bragg so greatly that he requested for a transfer out of Bragg's department in July and was replaced by D.H. Hill, brother-in-law to Stonewall Jackson and a close friend to both James Longstreet and Joseph E. Johnston. Although his military ability was well respected, he was underutilized during the second half of the Civil War due to his own falling out with Lee. Longstreet would later incur the wrath of some of his former Confederate comrades by writing that Hill was not given command of a corps in the Army of Northern Virginia because he wasn't a Virginian, which was considered an implicit criticism of Lee. Hill and Longstreet were both substantial command upgrades and among the best generals the Confederacy had, and by the time Chickamauga was over they would both harbor an intense dislike of Bragg as well.

Hill would write an account of the battle after the war that was published in the seminal *Battles & Leaders of the Civil War* series, and in it he recounted his first meeting with Bragg in years:

"On the 19th of July I reported to General Bragg at Chattanooga. I had not seen him since I had been the junior lieutenant in his battery of artillery at Corpus Christi, Texas, in 1845. The other two lieutenants were George H. Thomas and John F. Reynolds. We four had been in the same mess there. Reynolds had been killed at Gettysburg twelve days before my new assignment. Thomas, the strongest and most pronounced Southerner of the four, was now Rosecrans's lieutenant. It was a strange casting of lots that three messmates of Corpus Christi should meet under such changed circumstances at Chickamauga.

My interview with General Bragg at Chattanooga was not satisfactory. He was silent and reserved and seemed gloomy and despondent. He had grown prematurely old since I saw him last, and showed much nervousness. His relations with his next in command (General Polk) and with some others of his subordinates were known not to be pleasant. His many retreats, too, had alienated the rank and file from him, or at least had taken away that enthusiasm which soldiers feel for the successful general, and which makes them obey his orders without question, and thus wins for him other successes. The one thing that a soldier never fails to understand is victory, and the commander who leads him to victory will be adored by him whether that victory has been won by skill or by blundering, by the masterly handling of a few troops against great odds, or by the awkward use of over whelming numbers."

Hill's account suggests that the issues between Bragg and his subordinates were so well-known that it was already coloring the attitudes of men who had not yet served under him. It's likely that the only reason this situation was allowed to fester for as long as it did is because Bragg and Jefferson Davis had been close friends since their days at West Point decades earlier. Davis's loyalty to his friends presented similar problems, as he had very obvious favorites among his generals, like Lee, Bragg, and Albert Sidney Johnston. At the same time, he constantly bickered with other generals in the field, notably Joseph E. Johnston, and the discord hurt the Southern cause, especially in the West. Even after Davis reluctantly removed Bragg from command out West, he would bring Bragg to Richmond to serve as a military advisor.

While the discord among the generals clearly didn't help matters, the reinforcements gave Bragg a numbers advantage over Rosecrans, a rare situation for a Confederate army during the war. With that, Bragg was determined to take offensive operations in late August and early September, as he had been urged to do by the Confederate government.

Bragg's account noted that one of the reasons he wanted to delay moving forward was because the geographical terrain made advancing difficult, and he had hoped that it would be Rosecrans who would be forced to move forward in that same area. Sure enough, Rosecrans was hoping to avoid doing just that, but he was also being pressed to conduct offensive operations by his government. Rosecrans would thus have to march his army through the Cumberland Plateau, which would disrupt his supply lines due to poor roads and a lack of resources in the vicinity, and when he was ordered forward by Henry "Old Brains" Halleck, the general-in-chief, he described the order as being full of "recklessness, conceit and malice."

Rosecrans had managed to outmaneuver Bragg earlier in 1863 without much fighting, and he hoped to do so again in the summer. His ambitious plan called for using part of his army to pin down Bragg north of Chattanooga while the rest of his army crossed the Tennessee River well downstream and then had space to march forward on a wide front and encircle Bragg in Chattanooga or compel him to evacuate.

Rosecrans had outlined an overly ambitious marching strategy, which was made all the more bewildering by the fact that he detailed the complex difficulties associated with the movements in his post-battle report:

> "It is evident from this description of the topography that to reach Chattanooga, or penetrate the country south of it, on the railroad, by crossing the Tennessee below Chattanooga was a difficult task. It was necessary to cross the Cumberland Mountains, with subsistence, ammunition, at least a limited supply of forage, and a bridge train; to cross Sand or Raccoon Mountains into Lookout Valley, then Lookout Mountain, and finally the lesser ranges, Missionary Ridge, if we went directly to Chattanooga, or Missionary Ridge, Pigeon Mountain, and Taylor s Ridge, if we struck the railroad at Dalton or south of it. The Valley of the Tennessee River, though several miles in breadth between the bases of the mountains, below Bridgeport, is not a broad, alluvial farming country, but full of barren oak ridges, sparsely settled, and but a small part of it under cultivation...

> The first step was to repair the Nashville and Chattanooga Railroad, to bring forward to Tullahoma, McMinnville, Decherd, and Winchester needful forage and subsistence, which it was impossible to transport from Murfreesborough to those points over the horrible roads which we encountered on our advance to Tullahoma. The next was to extend the repairs of the main stem to Stevenson and Bridgeport, and the Tracy City branch, so that we could place supplies in depot at those points, from which to draw after we had crossed the mountains...

> The crossing of the river required that the best points should be chosen, and means provided for the crossing. The river was reconnoitered, the pontoons and trains ordered forward as rapidly as possible, hidden from view in rear of Stevenson and prepared for use. By the time they were ready the places of crossing had been selected and dispositions made to begin the operation.

> It was very desirable to conceal to the last moment the points of crossing, but as the mountains on the south side of the Tennessee rise in precipitous rocky bluffs to the height of 800 or 1,000 feet, completely overlooking the whole valley and its coves, this was next to impossible."

As Rosecrans was attempting the multiple crossings and aiming to concentrate his army again after doing so, the amount of time it took allowed more Confederate reinforcements to arrive from Mississippi. Adding to his challenges, there were only three suitable roads that could be used to link the several corps of his armies back together, leaving the isolated elements of his army dangerously exposed. When Bragg became aware of these dispositions, he evacuated from Chattanooga and fell back for the purpose of crushing that part of the Army of the Cumberland to his south, which included Alexander McCook's XX Corps and George H. Thomas's XIV Corps. Badly mistaking Bragg's movement as a general retreat further back into Atlanta, a joyous Rosecrans telegraphed Washington on September 9, "Chattanooga is ours without a struggle and East Tennessee is free."

Thomas

In actuality, Bragg had pulled the Army of Tennessee 20 miles back to LaFayette, which would allow him to potentially fall on the two isolated Union corps, who were way too far away from the rest of the Army of the Cumberland to receive support from them in the case of an attack. After Thomas Crittenden's XXI Corps occupied Chattanooga, Rosecrans ignored Thomas's advice to delay an advance on Bragg's army until the three Union corps could get within supporting range of each other and secure their supply lines. Instead, Rosecrans ordered one of his cavalry divisions to raid the Confederate supply lines at Resaca, have McCook's XX Corps swing further south across Lookout Mountain, push Crittenden's corps south in chase of Bragg, and move Thomas forward to LaFayette.

In other words, Rosecrans was unwittingly marching Thomas's 23,000 men straight at Bragg's entire army, just as Bragg was concentrating there for the purposes of attacking an isolated corps.

Chapter 2: Davis's Cross Roads

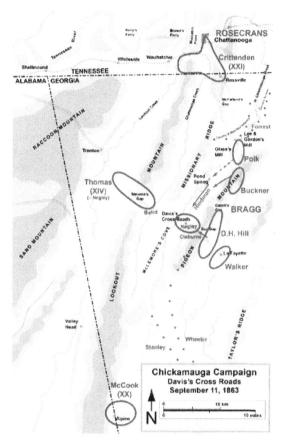

Chickamauga Campaign
Davis's Cross Roads
September 11, 1863

Given Rosecrans's orders, Thomas's corps began marching toward Dug Gap in column formation, with James Negley's division in the vanguard 12 hours ahead of the next closest division. Bragg was already aware of this forward movement on September 9, and he immediately took steps to attack Negley's division near Davis's Cross Roads by hopefully having Thomas Hindman's division march into Negley's rear near McLemore's Cove as Negley unwittingly pressed forward, thereby separating Negley from the rest of Thomas's corps:

"During the 9th it was ascertained that a column, estimated at from 4,000 to 8,000, had crossed Lookout Mountain into the cove by way of Stevens' and Cooper's Gaps. Thrown off his guard by our rapid movement, apparently in retreat, when in reality we had concentrated opposite his center, and deceived by the information from deserters and others sent into his lines, the enemy pressed on his columns to intercept us and thus exposed himself in detail.

Major-General Hindman received verbal instructions on the 9th to prepare his division to move against this force, and was informed that another division from Lieutenant-General Hill's command, at La Fayette, would join him. That evening the following written orders were issued to Generals Hindman and Hill:"

The first of several examples of incompetence among Confederate officers took place on the morning of September 10. Bragg had coordinated Hindman's division to march southwest into Negley's flank and rear as Patrick Cleburne's division of D.H. Hill's corps opposed Negley in front. As Negley kept unwittingly walking into the trap, around the time his division reached Davis's Cross Roads he heard about Hindman's movement threatening his left flank and rear and thus pulled back to take up a defensive position around McLemore's Cove, where Hindman could not flank him.

That countermarch was made possible by the fact that Cleburne's division never marched that day, which would lead to finger pointing between Bragg and D.H. Hill. Writing after the war, Hill blamed Bragg, insisting not only that the orders arrived too late but that Cleburne was ill and their proposed march would have been obstructed by physical obstacles anyway:

"As the failure of Bragg to beat Rosecrans in detail has been the subject of much criticism, it may be well to look into the causes of the failure. So far as the commanding general was concerned, the trouble with him was : first, lack of knowledge of the situation; second, lack of personal supervision of the execution of his orders. No general ever won a permanent fame who was wanting in these and elements of success, knowledge of his own and his enemy's condition, and personal superintendence of operations on the field.

The failure to attack Negley's division in the cove on September 10th, was owing to Bragg's ignorance of the condition of the roads, the obstructions at Dug Gap, and the position of the enemy."

D.H. Hill

While Hill dithered, Hindman had come within 4 miles of Negley's division but became concerned about attacking without Cleburne's division attacking in front as well. Even after being reinforced with more men from Buckner's corps, Hindman refused to make the attack on the afternoon of the 10th.

Infuriating Bragg even further, despite Hill's claims about Cleburne being sick, Cleburne was apparently well enough to order his division to start clearing the felled timber around Dug Gap and get ready to advance once he heard Hindman commence an attack on the 11th, but there seemed to have been some confusion at Hindman's headquarters over whether he was supposed to attack on the 11th. Hindman had already advised against making his attack on the 10th, only to have that advice rejected by Bragg, so naturally his attack on the 11th would be half-hearted as well. By the time the Confederates had finally coordinated an attack on Negley, a second division of the corps had reached them and taken up a defensive position, making an orderly retreat possible with a rearguard covering against Hindman's skirmishers.

Rosecrans seemed to more fully understand the situation and his dire predicament after the near disaster at Davis's Cross Roads, writing:

"On the 10th, Negley's division advanced to within a mile of Dug Gap, which he found heavily obstructed, and Baird's division came up to his support on the morning of the 11th. Negley became satisfied that the enemy was advancing upon him, in heavy force, and perceiving that if he accepted battle in that position he would probably be cut off, he fell back after a sharp skirmish, in which General Baird's division participated, skillfully covering and securing their trains, to a strong position in front of Stevens' Gap. On the 12th, Reynolds and Brannan, under orders to move promptly, closed up to the support of these two advanced divisions.

During the same day General McCook had reached the vicinity of Alpine, and, with infantry and cavalry, had reconnoitered the Broom-town Valley to Summerville, and ascertained that the enemy had not retreated on Rome, but was concentrating at La Fayette.

Thus it was ascertained that the enemy was concentrating all his forces, both infantry and cavalry, behind the Pigeon Mountain, in the vicinity of La Fayette, while the corps of this army were at Gordon's Mills, Bailey's Cross-Roads, at the foot of Stevens' Gap, and at Alpine, a distance of 40 miles, from flank to flank, by the nearest practicable roads, and 57 miles by the route subsequently taken by the Twentieth Army Corps. It had already been ascertained that the main body of Johnston's army had joined Bragg, and an accumulation of evidence showed that the troops from Virginia had reached Atlanta on the 1st of the month, and that re-enforcements were expected soon to arrive from that quarter. It was therefore a matter of life and death to effect the concentration of the army."

Chapter 3: Concentrating the Army of the Cumberland

The day after Negley avoided disaster in the south, Rosecrans began drawing up orders to link up his army. On September 12, he ordered McCook's XX Corps and his cavalry to march northeast and link up with Thomas's corps near Stevens Gap, and together they would continue marching northeast to link back up with Crittenden. As it turned out, the sheer distance between McCook and Rosecrans near Chattanooga meant it would take an entire day just for that order to reach McCook. It would then take at least three more days of hard marching to successfully link the three corps back up together.

Bragg's attempt to bag Negley's division had been a disappointment, but he still hoped to strike out at the isolated Union corps in detail, including Crittenden's corps. One of Bragg's cavalry corps, commanded by the legendary Nathan Bedford Forrest, reported Crittenden's southern movement toward Lee and Gordon's Mill, inducing Bragg to order Polk to make an attack with two of the corps under his command.

Forrest

On the night of September 12, Polk sent the order:

"Lieutenant-General POLK:

GENERAL: I inclose you a dispatch from General Pegram. This presents you a fine opportunity of striking Crittenden in detail, and I hope you will avail yourself of it at daylight to-morrow. This division crushed, and the others are yours. We can then turn again on the force in the cove. Wheeler's cavalry will move on Wilder, so as to cover your right. I shall be delighted to hear of your success."

Once again, the attack Bragg envisioned failed to materialize, this time because Bragg himself was unfamiliar with the dispositions of Crittenden's corps. Bragg had ordered Polk's men to certain points previously that would have made it impossible to reach Lee and Gordon's Mill in time to attack Crittenden before the entire corps had passed that point. This was lost on Bragg, who was infuriated at the time and complained in his post-battle report:

"Early on the 13th, I proceeded to the front, ahead of Buckner's command, to find that no advance had been made on the enemy, and that his forces had formed a junction and recrossed the Chickamauga. Again disappointed, immediate measures were taken to place our trains and limited supplies in safe positions, when all our forces were concentrated along the Chickamauga, threatening the enemy in front."

D.H. Hill pinned the blame for Bragg's lack of knowledge on what he considered a very obvious mistake, juxtaposing him with Stonewall Jackson for good measure:

"During the active operations of a campaign the post of the commander-in-chief should be in the center of his marching columns, that he may be able to give prompt and efficient aid to whichever wing may be threatened. But whenever a great battle is to be fought, the commander must be on the field to see that his orders are executed and to take advantage of the ever-changing phases of the conflict. Jackson leading a cavalry fight by night near Front Royal in the pursuit of Banks, Jackson at the head of the column following McClellan in the retreat from Richmond to Malvern Hill, presents a contrast to Bragg sending, from a distance of ten miles, four consecutive orders for an attack at daylight, which he was never to witness.

Surely in the annals of warfare there is no parallel to the coolness and nonchalance with which General Crittenden marched and counter-marched for a week with a delightful unconsciousness that he was in the presence of a force of superior strength. On the 11 we find him with two divisions (Van Cleve's and Palmer's) at Ringgold, twenty miles from Chattanooga, and with his third (Thomas J. Wood's), ten miles from Ringgold, at Lee and Gordon's Mills where it remained alone and unsupported, until late in the , day of the 12th."

Over the next several days, Rosecrans began to concentrate his army relatively unmolested and try to bring them all safely back toward Chattanooga. For their part, Bragg and his commanders decided that attacking Rosecrans in or around Chattanooga was their best available option. By the time that decision was made, the two divisions of Longstreet's corps that had been detached were just days away from arriving by rail.

On September 17, McCook's corps and Thomas's corps had linked back up, but Bragg tried to strike out north on September 18 toward Chattanooga, hoping to force a battle with Rosecrans or take the valuable city unopposed. If the Army of the Cumberland did put up a fight, Bragg figured his men would be well-positioned to turn their left flank, but in so doing he issued complex orders that would require a nearly impossible degree of coordination at 4 distinct crossing points of the Chickamauga creek.

"HEADQUARTERS ARMY OF TENNESSEE,

In the Field, Leet's Tan-yard, September 18, 1863.

1. Johnson's column (Hood's), on crossing at or near Reed's Bridge, will turn to the left by the most practicable route and sweep up the Chickamauga, toward Leo and Gordon's Mills.

2. Walker, crossing at Alexander's Bridge, will unite in this move and push vigorously on the enemy's flank and rear in the same direction.

3. Buckner, crossing at Thedford's Ford, will join in the movement to the left, and press the enemy up the stream from Polk's front at Lee and Gordon's Mills.

4. Polk will press his forces to the front of Lee and Gordon's Mills, and if met by too much resistance to cross will bear to the right and cross at Dalton's Ford, or at Thedford's, as may be necessary, and join in the attack wherever the enemy may be.

5. Hill will cover our left flank from an advance of the enemy from the cove, and by pressing the cavalry in his front ascertain if the enemy is re-enforcing at Lee and-Gordon's Mills, in which event he will attack them in flank.

6. Wheeler's cavalry will hold the gaps in Pigeon Mountain and cover our rear and left and bring up stragglers.

7. All teams, &c., not with troops should go toward Ringgold and Dalton, beyond Taylor's Ridge. All cooking should be done at the trains. Rations, when cooked, will be forwarded to the troops.

8. The above movements wall be executed with the utmost promptness, vigor, and persistence."

Naturally, these movements were full of delays on the morning of the 18th, not to mention the presence of Union cavalry in the area. Bragg later reported, "The resistance offered by the enemy's cavalry and the difficulties arising from the bad and narrow country roads caused unexpected delays in the execution of these movements. Though the commander of the right column was several times urged to press forward, his crossing was not effected until late in the afternoon."

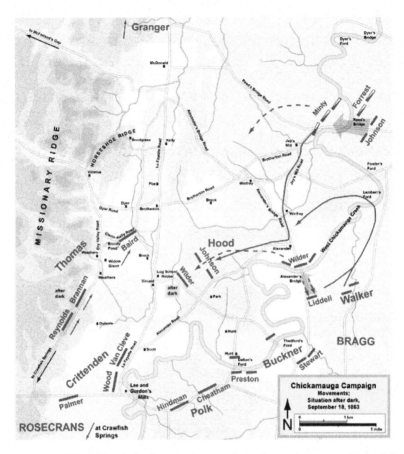

Rosecrans correctly predicted what Bragg was attempting and moved to counter it by quickly bringing up Thomas on Crittenden's left:

"Evidence accumulated during the day of the 18th that the enemy was moving to our left. Minty's cavalry and Wilder's mounted brigade encountered the enemy's cavalry at Reed's and Alexander's Bridges, and toward evening were driven into the Rossville road. At the same time the enemy had been demonstrating for 3 miles up the Chickamauga. Heavy clouds of dust had been observed 3 or 4 miles beyond the Chickamauga, sweeping to the northeast.

In view of all these facts, the necessity became apparent that General Thomas must use all possible dispatch in moving his corps to the position assigned it. He was therefore directed to proceed with all dispatch, and General McCook to close up to Crawfish Spring as soon as Thomas' column was out of the way. Thomas pushed forward uninterruptedly during the night, and at daylight the head of his column had reached Kelly's house on the La Fayette road, where Baird's division was posted. Brannan followed, and was posted on Baird's left, covering the roads leading to Reed's and Alexander's Bridges.

General Thomas ordered Brannan with two brigades to reconnoiter in that direction and attack any small force he should meet. The advance brigade, supported by the rest of the division, soon encountered a strong body of the enemy, attacked it vigorously, and drove it back more than half a mile, where a very strong column of the enemy was found, with the evident intention of turning our left and gaining possession of the La Fayette road between us and Chattanooga."

After the delays and dealing with the advanced Union defenders, several of Bragg's divisions had successfully pushed across the Chickamauga. By now, however, Thomas and Crooks were within supporting distance of Crittenden's corps. D.H. Hill faulted Bragg for being too late to make his attack orders:

"Had this order been issued on any of the four preceding days, it would have found Rosecrans wholly unprepared for it, with but a single infantry division (Wood's) guarding the crossings of the Chickamauga, and that at one point only, Lee and Gordon's - the fords north of it being watched by cavalry . Even if the order had been given twenty-four hours earlier, it must have been fatal to Rosecrans in the then huddled and confused grouping of his forces.

All that was effected on the 18th was the sending over of Walker's small corps of a little more than 5000 men near Alexander's Bridge, and Bushrod Johnson's division of 3600 men at Reed's Bridge, farther north. These troops drove off Wilder's mounted infantry from the crossings immediately south of them, so as to leave undisputed passage for Bragg's infantry, except in the neighborhood of Lee and Gordon's."

Chapter 4: September 19

Bragg's attack hadn't been carried out as expeditiously as he had hoped, but because he was unaware of the location of Thomas's corps, he planned for yet another attack on what he believed to be the Union's left flank during the morning of the 19th:

"The movement was resumed at daylight on the 19th, and Buckner's corps, with Cheatham's division, of Polk's, had crossed and formed, when a brisk engagement commenced with our cavalry under Forrest on the extreme right about 9 o'clock. A brigade from Walker was ordered to Forrest's support, and soon after Walker was ordered to attack with his whole force. Our line was now formed, with Buckner's left resting on the Chickamauga about 1 mile below Lee and Gordon's Mills. On his right came Hood with his own and Johnson's divisions, with Walker on the extreme right, Cheatham's division being in reserve, the general direction being a little east of north. The attack ordered by our right was made by General Walker in his usual gallant style, and soon developed a largely superior force opposed."

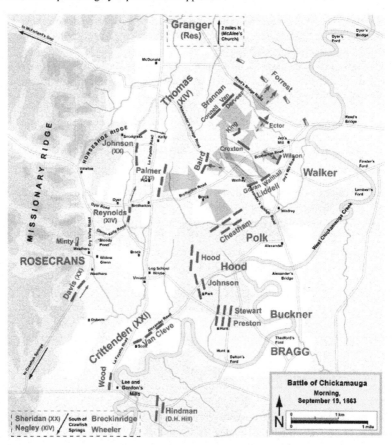

Fighting on the morning of September 19

Ironically, the first fighting of what became the Battle of Chickamauga involved Forrest's cavalry skirmishing with advanced pickets from Army of the Cumberland's Reserve Corps, commanded by Gordon Granger and stationed a couple of miles north. While those forces skirmished, it provided the Confederates evidence of the fact that the Union's left flank was not nearly as far south as Bragg had assumed it was. As the Union pickets were withdrawn north, the commander of their brigade, Daniel McCook, reported to Thomas that he assumed the fighting meant a Confederate infantry brigade was across the Chickamauga and potentially isolated. Unsure of whether McCook's report was accurate, Thomas sent orders to one of his division commanders, John Brannan, to try to find the brigade and destroy it. Thomas later reported:

"I directed General Brannan to post a brigade, within supporting distance of Baird, on the road to Alexander's Bridge, and with his other two brigades to reconnoiter the road leading to Reed's Bridge to see if he could locate the brigade reported by Colonel McCook, and, if a favorable opportunity occurred, to capture it. His dispositions were made according to instructions by 9 a.m."

McCook, of course, had skirmished with Forrest's Confederate cavalry, not a vulnerable infantry brigade. As the Union division advanced in a battle line, Forrest fought a delaying action by dismounting his cavalry troopers while requesting reinforcements from Bragg and William Walker, the commander of the two-division corps just south of Forrest's troopers. While Walker was ordering one of his brigades forward around 9:00 a.m., Bragg interpreted the advance of Brannan's division as being a major attack on his right flank, so he began the process of scrambling more and more men to his right. Thus, Thomas thought he was dealing with a Confederate brigade and had sent a division, while Bragg thought he was dealing with a major offensive by Rosecrans. Bragg later reported, "The enemy, whose left was at Lee and Gordon's Mills when our movement commenced, had rapidly transferred forces from his extreme right, changing his entire line, and seemed disposed to dispute with all his ability our effort to gain the main road to Chattanooga, in his rear. Lieutenant-General Polk was ordered to move his remaining division across at the nearest ford, and to assume the command in person on our right. Hill's corps was also ordered to cross below Lee and Gordon's Mills and join the line on the right."

By the time those movements were being made by the Confederates, the fighting between Walker's brigade and Forrest's cavalry against Brannan's division had started in earnest. Even by this early point, it was clear that the terrain around the Chickamauga would play a major role in the nature of the fighting and the ability to control the armies. Historian Steven Woodworth aptly described its effects on the fighting:

"The land between Chickamauga Creek and the LaFayette Road was gently rolling but almost completely wooded. ... In the woods no officer above brigadier could see all his command at once, and even the brigadiers often could see nobody's troops but their own and perhaps the enemy's. Chickamauga would be a classic 'soldiers battle,' but it would test officers at every level of command in ways they had not previously been tested. An additional complication was that each army would be attempting to fight a shifting battle while shifting its own position...Each general would have to conduct a battle while shuffling his own units northward toward an enemy of whose position he could get only the vaguest idea. Strange and wonderful opportunities would loom out of the leaves, vines, and gunsmoke, be touched and vaguely sensed, and then fade away again into the figurative fog of confusion that bedeviled men on both sides. In retrospect, victory for either side would look simple when unit positions were reviewed on a neat map, but in Chickamauga's torn and smoky woodlands, nothing was simple."

As the fighting started raging between Brannan's division and the Confederates, it acted like a vacuum that began sucking in nearby units on both sides, as Thomas started ordering more of his men to relieve Brannan. Thomas reported:

"General Baird was directed to throw forward his right wing, so as to get more nearly in line with Brannan, but to watch well on his right flank. Soon after this disposition of those two divisions, a portion of Palmer's division, of Crittenden's corps, took position to the right of General Baird's division. About 10 o'clock Croxton's brigade of Brannan's division, posted on the road leading to Alexander's Bridge, became engaged with the enemy, and I rode forward to his position to ascertain the character of the attack. Colonel Croxton reported to me that he had driven the enemy nearly half a mile, but that he was then meeting with obstinate resistance. I then rode back to Baird's position, and directed him to advance to Croxton's support, which he did with his whole division, Starkweather's brigade in reserve, and drove the enemy steadily before him for some distance, taking many prisoners. Croxton's brigade, which had been heavily engaged for over an hour with greatly superior numbers of the enemy, and being nearly exhausted of ammunition, was then moved to the rear to enable the men to fill up their boxes; and Baird and Brannan, having united their forces, drove the enemy from their immediate front. General Baird then halted for the purpose of readjusting his line; and hearing from prisoners that the enemy were in heavy force on his immediate right, he threw back his right wing in order to be ready for an attack from that quarter."

As Baird's division was pushing the Confederates back, St. John R. Liddell's division arrived to reinforce the Confederate line, hitting Baird's right flank and routing them. However, as Baird's brigades were breaking for the rear, the advancing Confederates were stunned and stopped by Ferdinand Van Derveer's brigade of Brannan's division. These attacks and counterattacks had inflicted steady losses, but neither side was able to hold onto the advantage for long, which all but guaranteed that both sides would send more men that way to try to achieve a decisive breakthrough.

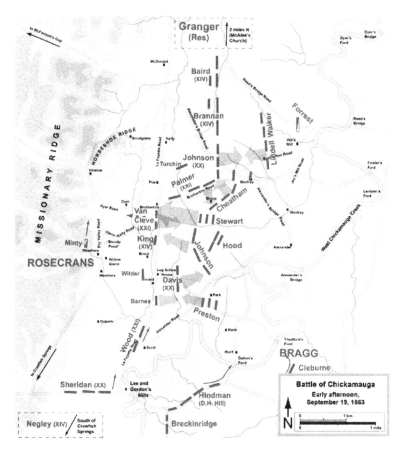

The fighting on the afternoon of September 19

The problem with this kind of fighting, as Hill noted, was that the reinforcements would go in piecemeal and make uncoordinated attacks, as opposed to reforming lines and making a general advance in larger force. Hill explained, "Unfortunately for the Confederates, there was no general advance, as there might have been along the whole line-an advance that must have given a more decisive victory on the 19th than was gained on the 20th. It was desultory fighting from right to left, without concert, and at inopportune times. It was the sparring of the amateur boxer, and not the crushing blows of the trained pugilist. From daylight on the 19th until after midday, there was a gap of two miles between Crittenden and Thomas, into which the Confederates could have poured, turning to right or left, and attacking in flank whichever commander was least prepared for the assault."

The closest the Confederates would come to a breakthrough would be in the center of the Union line during the early afternoon by men under the command of tenacious Texan John Bell Hood. A division commander in Longstreet's corps, Hood had been severely wounded at Gettysburg, recovering in time for the fighting at Chickamauga, and until Longstreet personally arrived later on the night of the 19th, Hood had command of the men in Longstreet's corps, which included his own division and Bushrod Johnson's division. As they advanced around 2:30, they began to steadily push the Union defenders back, thereby relieving a Confederate division under Alexander Stewart on their right, and for a moment they took control of the road to Chattanooga. However, a further advance was rebuffed by reinforcements in the form of four Union divisions, which pushed them back across the road, ensuring the Army of the Cumberland could keep using it to keep its own corps together.

Hood

The Union army subsequently launched a series of unsuccessful and uncoordinated counterattacks in that same sector, failing to push back the three Confederate divisions that had made about a mile of progress. Those attacks came to an end as night fell, but Bragg still intended to keep the fight going that night. Around 6:00 p.m., as it was getting dark, Bragg ordered Cleburne's division to shore up the Confederate army's right flank. Though the fighting in that sector had died down as Hood's men had pushed the action to the south, Cleburne now launched an attack that was hampered by the night and the heavily wooded underbrush. Cleburne called off the attack at 9:00 p.m., but not before having incurred about 30% casualties in his division.

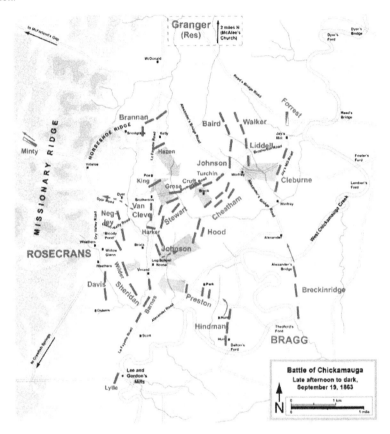

The last attacks of September 19

At the end of the fighting on September 19, some of the Confederates felt they had won a victory, particularly Bragg and Hood. Bragg was also determined to take the fight to Rosecrans again the following day:

"Night found us masters of the ground, after a series of very obstinate contests with largely superior numbers. From captured prisoners and others we learned with certainty that we had encountered the enemy's whole force, which had been moving day and night since they first ascertained the direction of our march. Orders had been given for the rapid march to the field of all re-enforcements arriving by railroad, and three additional brigades from this source joined us early next morning. The remaining forces on our extreme left, east of the Chickamauga, had been ordered up early in the afternoon, but reached the field too late to participate in the engagement of that day. They were ordered into line on their arrival, and disposed for a renewal of the action early the next morning."

Naturally, Rosecrans saw things differently, reporting:

"The roar of battle hushed in the darkness of night, and our troops, weary with a night of marching and a day of fighting, rested on their arms, having everywhere maintained their positions, developed the enemy, and gained thorough command of the Rossville and Dry Valley roads to Chattanooga, the great object of the battle of the 19th of September.

The battle had secured us these objects. Our flanks covered the Dry Valley and Rossville roads, while our cavalry covered the Missionary Ridge and the Valley of Chattanooga Creek, into which latter place our spare trains had been sent on Friday, the 18th.

We also had indubitable evidence of the presence of Longstreet's corps and Johnston's forces, by the capture of prisoners from each, and the fact that at the close of the day we had present but two brigades which had not been opportunely and squarely in action, opposed to superior numbers of the enemy, assured us that we were greatly outnumbered, and that the battle the next day must be for the safety of the army and the possession of Chattanooga."

To a degree, both of them were partly wrong. Rosecrans had not been attacked by a greatly superior force, but he was right that the Army of the Cumberland certainly hadn't suffered any consequential setbacks either. Both men have been criticized for the nature of the attacks and the counterattacks, which inflicted thousands of casualties on each other through piecemeal actions that only involved individual brigades or divisions, as opposed to concerted attacks with multiple divisions or a corps.

Bragg has been particularly criticized by historians for the failure to win anything of substance on the 19th. Thomas Connelly, who wrote a history on the Confederate Army of Tennessee, asserted, "Bragg's inability to readjust his plans had cost him heavily. He had never admitted that he was wrong about the location of Rosecrans' left wing and that as a result he bypassed two splendid opportunities. During the day Bragg might have sent heavy reinforcements to Walker and attempted to roll up the Union left; or he could have attacked the Union center where he knew troops were passing from to the left. Unable to decide on either, Bragg tried to do both, wasting his men in sporadic assaults. Now his Army was crippled and in no better position than that morning. Walker had, in the day's fighting, lost over 20 per cent of his strength, while Stuart and Cleburne had lost 30 per cent. Gone, too, was any hope for the advantage of a surprise blow against Rosecrans."

On top of that, Bragg's previous defeats had sapped the morale of the Confederate army and their belief in his abilities, something Hood noticed on the night of the 19th. Hood later noted in his memoirs, "In the evening, according to my custom in Virginia under General Lee, I rode back to Army headquarters to report to the Commander-in-Chief the result of the day upon my part of the line. I there met for the first time several of the principal officers of the Army of Tennessee, and, to my surprise, not one spoke in a sanguine tone regarding the result of the battle in which we were then engaged. I found the gallant Breckinridge, whom I had known from early youth, seated by the root of a tree, with a heavy slouch hat upon his head. When, in the course of brief conversation, I stated that we would rout the enemy the following day, he sprang to his feet, exclaiming, 'My dear Hood, I am delighted to hear you say so. You give me renewed hope; God grant it may be so.'"

One thing may have gone right for the Confederates on the night of the 19th. As Longstreet and his men marched toward Bragg's army, they may have inadvertently run into the Union army. Longstreet explained the odd encounter in his memoirs:

It was a bright moonlight night, and the woodlands on the sides of the broad highway were quite open, so that we could see and be seen. After a time we were challenged by an outlying guard, 'Who comes there?' We answered, 'Friends.' The answer was not altogether satisfying to the guard, and after a very short parley we asked what troops they were, when the answer gave the number of the brigade and of the division. As Southern brigades were called for their commanders more than by their numbers, we concluded that these friends were the enemy. There were, too, some suspicious obstructions across the road in front of us, and altogether the situation did not look inviting. The moon was so bright that it did not seem prudent to turn and ride back under the fire that we knew would be opened on us, so I said, loudly, so that the guard could hear, 'Let us ride down a little way to find a better crossing.' Riding a few rods brought us under cover and protection of large trees, sufficiently shading our retreat to enable us to ride quietly to the rear and take the road over which we had seen so many men and vehicles passing while on our first ride."

Surprisingly, by the time Longstreet and his men arrived around 11:00 p.m., Bragg was asleep. It was then that Longstreet learned he was being given command of the left wing of the army, leaving Hood in command of his corps, and that Leonidas Polk was given command of the right wing of the army.

Bragg's decision to reorganize his command structure ahead of the attack on the 20th has also come in for criticism, especially because it confused some of his own officers by adding another layer of command for orders. This was particularly a problem for the Confederates' right flank, which was manned by the corps of D.H. Hill. It was not until late that night that Hill even learned about the reorganization of the command structure, and that he had now been made one of Polk's subordinates. And if Hill is to be believed, the confusion that resulted in the reorganization led to him not receiving the attack orders that Bragg intended for him on the morning of the 20th:

> "[M]y chief-of-staff gave me a message from General Polk that my corps had been put under his command, and that he wished to see me at Alexander's Bridge. He said not a word to any of them about an attack at daylight, nor did he to General Breckinridge, who occupied the same room with him that night. I have by me written statements from General Breckinridge and the whole of my staff to that effect. General Polk had issued an order for an attack at daylight, and had sent a courier with a copy, but he had failed to find me. I saw the order for the first time nineteen years afterward in Captain Polk's letter to the Southern Historical Society."

Chapter 5: The Morning of September 20

"Taken as a whole, the performance of the Confederate right wing this morning had been one of the most appalling exhibitions of command incompetence of the entire Civil War." – Steven Woodworth

On the morning of the 20th, Bragg had anticipated that his right flank would be launching an attack on the Union left at daylight, only to discover nothing going on at daylight. Bragg reported:

> "Lieutenant-General Polk was ordered to assail the enemy on our extreme right at day-dawn on the 20th, and to take up the attack in succession rapidly to the left. The left wing was to await the attack by the right, take it up promptly when made, and the whole line was then to be pushed vigorously and persistently against the enemy throughout its extent.
>
> Before the dawn of day myself and staff were ready for the saddle, occupying a position immediately in rear of and accessible to all parts of the Free. With increasing anxiety and disappointment I waited until after sunrise without hearing a gun, and at length dispatched a staff officer to Lieutenant-General Polk to ascertain the cause of the delay and urge him to a prompt and speedy movement. This officer, not finding the general with his troops, and learning where he had spent the night, proceeded across Alexander's Bridge to the east side of the Chickamauga and there delivered my message.
>
> Proceeding in person to the right wing, I found the troops not even prepared for the

movement. Messengers were immediately dispatched for Lieutenant-General Polk, and he shortly after joined me. My orders were renewed, and the general was urged to their prompt execution, the more important as the ear was saluted throughout the night with the sounds of the ax and falling timber as the enemy industriously labored to strengthen his position by hastily constructed barricades and breastworks. A reconnaissance made in the front of our extreme right during this delay crossed the main road to Chattanooga and proved the important fact that this greatly desired position was open to our possession."

When Bragg found Hill around 8:00 a.m., Hill later claimed that was the first time he had heard of an attack order, after which he protested to Bragg that an attack would be unwise:

"Bragg rode up at 8 A. M. and inquired of me why I had not begun the attack at daylight. I told him that I was hearing then for the first time that such an order had been issued and had not known whether we were to be the assailants or the assailed. He said angrily, 'I found Polk after sunrise sitting down reading a newspaper at Alexander's Bridge, two miles from the line of battle, where he ought to have been fighting.' However, the essential preparations for battle had not been made up to this hour and, in fact, could not be made without the presence of the commander-in-chief. The position of the enemy had not been reconnoitered, our line of battle had not been adjusted, and par t of it was at right angles with the rest; there was no cavalry on our flanks, and no order had fixed the strength or position of the reserves."

The delay may have been fatal. Around 9:30 a.m., 4 hours after Bragg intended for the attack on the Union left to start, with Breckinridge's division and Cleburne's division of Hill's corps pushing forward. This was problematic for several reasons. First, Bragg intended that Cleburne and Breckinridge would be just the start of a coordinated series of attacks that would drive the Union's left flank to the south and southwest. Second, the delay allowed Thomas's men to dig in and erect breastworks that would greatly aid their defensive line, leading Bragg to complain that without the Confederates' delay, "our independence might have been won.

Perhaps most important of all, Bragg's attack was starting with a division that had fought late the previous night and had been sapped of nearly a third of its manpower. While Breckinridge's division had some success on the far right of the line and began pushing south along the LaFayette Road, the presence of Union breastworks had discouraged some of his men and the men in Cleburne's division. Cleburne's men went nowhere in front of several Union divisions, and the left wing of his division got mixed up with Stewart's division, which had marched to the right to close a gap in the Confederate line and inadvertently marched into the left wing of Cleburne's division. Since Stewart and Cleburne had their men tangled, Benjamin Cheatham's division, poised to advance after them, could not move forward with the Confederates in their front. Meanwhile, Hill's attempt to shore up the gap forming between Breckinridge and Cleburne was quickly savaged, and the gap remained in the line.

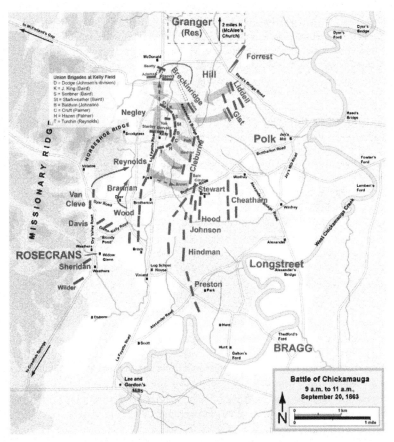

The Confederate attacks on the morning of September 20

By noon, the attack that Bragg had envisioned starting at dawn and rolling up the Union's left flank had completely fizzled out. Bragg could not hide his disgust in his official report, writing:

"The reasons assigned for this unfortunate delay by the wing commander appear in part in the reports of his subordinates. It is sufficient to say they are entirely unsatisfactory. It also appears from these reports that when the action was opened on the right about 10 a.m. the troops were moved to the assault in detail and by detachments, unsupported, until nearly all parts of the right wing were in turn repulsed with heavy losses.

Our troops were led with the greatest gallantry and exhibited great coolness, bravery, and heroic devotion. In no instance did they fail when called on to rally and return to the charge. But though invariably driving the enemy with slaughter at the points assailed, they were compelled in turn to yield to the greatly superior numbers constantly brought against them."

Chapter 6: The Union Blunder

The only good thing that can be said about the Confederates' attack on the morning of September 20 is that it set in motion a chain of miscommunications among Union officers that would ultimately produce one of the biggest blunders of the entire war.

When the attack started on the left flank, Thomas began requesting reinforcements from the generals and commands to his right. One of them was Brannan, and he sent a brigade north as reinforcements early in the morning only to be asked for more reinforcements around 10:00 a.m. At the same time, Brannan was aware that if he sent his entire division as reinforcements, it would leave a gap between Thomas Wood's division and Joseph Reynolds's division, so he initially talked the matter over with Reynolds, who suggested that Brannan withdraw his division but only after informing Rosecrans back at headquarters.

Brannan

Brannan wisely kept his division in the line, prudently waiting for Rosecrans to approve the decision and giving Rosecrans time to then reform the line and close up the gap. But somehow,

Brannan's staff officer got the notion that Brannan's division was in the process of pulling out of the line and marching north as he rode back to Rosecrans. Rosecrans explained, "A message from General Thomas soon followed, that he was heavily pressed, Captain Kellogg, aide-de-camp, the bearer, informing me at the same time that General Brannan was out of line, and General Reynolds' right was exposed. Orders were dispatched to General Wood to close up on Reynolds, and word was sent to General Thomas that he should be supported, even if it took away the whole corps of Crittenden and McCook. General Davis was ordered to close on General Wood, and General McCook was advised of the state of affairs and ordered to close his whole command to the left with all dispatch."

The orders that Wood received were not what Rosecrans remembered, probably because Rosecrans did not actually review the orders before they reached Wood. Instead, his aide-de-camp, Frank Bond, wrote out the order to Wood: "The general commanding directs that you close up on Reynolds as fast as possible, and support him." Since Brannan's division was still in line, Wood could not "close up" on Reynolds's right because that spot was already filled. To "support" Reynolds meant that Wood should pull his division and organize in the rear of Reynolds's division. In other words, there was no way Wood could close up and support Reynolds at the same time unless Brannan's division had already moved out of the line.

Since it was impossible to close up on Reynolds, Wood decided to go ahead and support Reynolds, thereby pulling his division out of the Union line. Wood knew full well that he was creating a gap and thought the orders were strange, but he had already been chastised for not moving promptly after receiving orders earlier that day, so he accepted the orders. Historian Peter Cozzens noted the argument over the intent of the orders between Wood and one of the staffers:

"While Wood read the order, Starling began to explain its intent. Wood interrupted. Brannan was in position, he said, there was no vacancy between Reynold's division and his own. 'Then there is no order,' retorted Starling. There the matter should have ended. And with anyone but Tom Wood, it most assuredly would have. Rosecrans had upbraided Wood twice for failing to obey orders promptly...the dressing down just 90 minutes earlier in front of Wood's entire staff. The barbs of Rosecrans's invective pained the Kentuckian. Anger clouded his reason. No, he told Starling, the order was imperative, he would move at once."

Instead of verifying the intent with Rosecrans, whose headquarters were just 5 minutes away, Wood began to act. As he began pulling his division out of the line, Wood did not consult with his own corps commander (Crittenden) but with corps commander McCook, and though Wood later claimed McCook vowed to fill the gap, the gap essentially went unfilled. Wood was pulling out an entire division from the line, and it would only be partially filled by a single brigade.

Wood

Thus, unbeknownst to Rosecrans and McCook, a wide gap was being created right in the middle of the right wing of the Army of the Cumberland's line, and as fortune would have it, the delays brought about by Confederate confusion on their right resulted in Longstreet's left wing delaying its own attack until after 11:00. Having taken time to reform his battle lines, Longstreet had established an attacking force in 5 lines consisting of three divisions with his veterans from the Army of Northern Virginia. Bushrod Johnson's division was in front, and it was given the objective of advancing across the field of the Brotherton farm, the very part of the line that Wood's division was vacating.

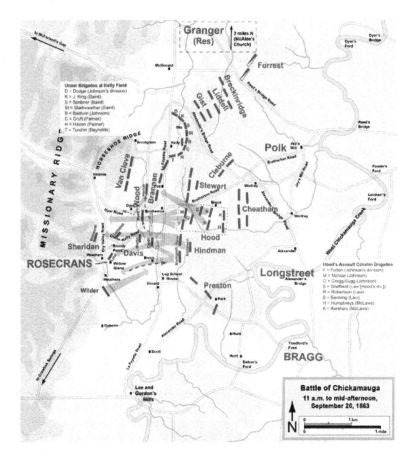

Longstreet's attack

Longstreet has often been criticized for being slow to march and form his lines before an attack, but there's no question that this time it was incredibly fortuitous. The initial attackers struck the right flank of Wood's division was it was pulling out of the line and routed them, establishing the gap for nearly 15,000 Confederates to push through. Longstreet described the initial rout in his memoirs:

"As we approached a second line, Johnson's division happened to strike it while in the act of changing position of some of the troops, charged upon and carried it, capturing some artillery, Hood's and Hindman's troops pressing in close connection. This attack forced the parts of the Twentieth and Twenty-first Corps from that part of the field, back over Missionary Ridge, in disordered retreat, and part of Negley's division of the Fourteenth Corps by the same impulsion. As our right wing had failed of the progress anticipated, and had become fixed by the firm holding of the enemy's left, we could find no practicable field for our work except by a change of the order of battle from wheel to the left, to a swing to the right on my division under General Stewart."

Bushrod Johnson was awed by the sight of the Confederates streaming through the gap, writing, "The scene now presented was unspeakably grand. The resolute and impetuous charge, the rush of our heavy columns sweeping out from the shadow and gloom of the forest into the open fields flooded with sunlight, the glitter of arms, the onward dash of artillery and mounted men, the retreat of the foe, the shouts of the hosts of our army, the dust, the smoke, the noise of fire-arms—of whistling balls and grape-shot and of bursting shell—made up a battle scene of unsurpassed grandeur."

By pushing through the gap and wheeling to the right, Longstreet had effectively cut the Army of the Cumberland in two and now fell upon the left flank of Crittenden's corps. Shortly after Longstreet's wheel to the right started, the man in charge of his corps, Hood, was nearly killed. Hood explained, "With a shout along my entire front, the Confederates rushed forward, penetrated into the wood, over and beyond the enemy's breastworks, and thus achieved another glorious victory for our arms. About this time I was pierced with a Minie ball in the upper third of the right leg; I turned from my horse upon the side of the crushed limb and fell — strange to say, since I was commanding five divisions — into the arms of some of the troops of my old brigade, which I had directed so long a period, and upon so many fields of battle." Hood's leg would be amputated nearly at the hip.

As several Union brigades began heading to the rear, one of the brigades in Wood's division, commanded by Charles Harker, managed to stay intact enough to withdraw in an orderly fashion toward Horseshoe Ridge, a naturally strong defensive spot. Luckily for Harker and the Union, the Confederates in his front, brigades led by Joseph Kershaw and Benjamin G. Humphreys, were unsupported in their advance and were unable to dislodge the brigade from Horseshoe Ridge. In the chaos and confusion, the Confederate brigades closest to Kershaw and Humphreys had become scattered in their pursuit of retreating Union brigades.

By driving through the gap and wheeling to the right, Longstreet's left flank was exposed to some of the divisions in McCook's XX Corps, but the general chaos and panic resulted in most of that corps putting up almost no fight and evacuating the field to the west. With command structure having entirely broken down, brigadier-generals were left to their own devices, and those that tried to stay and fight were dispatched by some of the Confederate attackers who had not wheeled left so as to protect the flank.

Little Phil Sheridan's division was a textbook example of the difficulties Union generals had in maintaining order. As two of his brigades, led by William Lytle and Nathan Walworth, held their ground and actually repulsed the Confederate advance, his other two brigades had quickly broken and fled to the rear. When Lytle was killed leading his men, the leaderless brigade also quickly broke. Sheridan would describe his situation in his memoirs:

"During these occurrences General Rosecrans passed down the road behind my line, and sent word that he wished to see me, but affairs were too critical to admit of my going to him at once, and he rode on to Chattanooga. It is to be regretted that he did not wait till I could join him, for the delay would have permitted him to see that matters were not in quite such bad shape as he supposed; still, there is no disguising the fact that at this juncture his army was badly crippled.

Shortly after my division had rallied on the low hills already described, I discovered that the enemy, instead of attacking me in front, was wedging in between my division and the balance of the army; in short, endeavoring to cut me off from Chattanooga. This necessitated another retrograde movement, which brought me back to the southern face of Missionary Ridge, where I was joined by Carlin's brigade of Davis's division. Still thinking I could join General Thomas, I rode some distance to the left of my line to look for a way out, but found that the enemy had intervened so far as to isolate me effectually. I then determined to march directly to Rossville, and from there effect ajunction with Thomas by the Lafayette road. I reached Rossville about 5 o'clock in the afternoon, bringing with me eight guns, forty-six caissons, and a long ammunition train, the latter having been found in a state of confusion behind the widow Glenn's when I was being driven back behind the Dry Valley road."

Rosecrans justified his leaving the field in his post-battle report:

"At the moment of the repulse of Davis' division, I was standing in rear of his right, waiting the completion of the closing of McCook's corps to the left. Seeing confusion among Van Cleve's troops, and the distance Davis' men were falling back, and the tide of battle surging toward us, the urgency for Sheridan's troops to intervene became imminent, and I hastened in person to the extreme right, to direct Sheridan's movement on the flank of the advancing rebels. It was too late. The crowd of returning troops rolled back, and the enemy advanced. Giving the troops directions to rally behind the ridge west of the Dry Valley road, I passed down it accompanied by General Garfield, Major McMichael, Major Bond, and Captain Young, of my staff, and a few of the escort, under a shower of grape, canister, and musketry, for 200 or 300 yards, and attempted to rejoin General Thomas and the troops sent to his support, by passing to the rear of the broken portion of our lines, but found the routed troops far toward the left, and hearing the enemy's advancing musketry and cheers, I became doubtful whether the left had held its ground, and started for Rossville. On consultation and further reflection, however, I determined to send General Garfield there, while I went to

Chattanooga, to give orders for the security of the pontoon bridges at Battle Creek and Bridgeport, and to make preliminary dispositions either to forward ammunition and supplies, should we hold our ground, or to withdraw the troops into good position."

However, Sheridan's sentiment about Rosecrans's disappearance was echoed by Rosecrans biographer William Lamers, who wrote, "Whether he did or did not know that Thomas still held the field, it was a catastrophe that Rosecrans did not himself ride to Thomas, and send Garfield to Chattanooga. Had he gone to the front in person and shown himself to his men, as at Stone River, he might by his personal presence have plucked victory from disaster, although it is doubtful whether he could have done more than Thomas did. Rosecrans, however, rode to Chattanooga instead."

Around the same time, one of the Union's cavalry brigades, led by John T. Wilder, was prevented from trying to attack Longstreet's flank by Assistant Secretary of War Charles Dana, who had grown so discouraged by what he had seen that he demanded to be taken back to Chattanooga, where he could inform Washington of what was going on via telegraph. Wilder had to detach part of his command to escort Dana to the city, and that afternoon Dana hysterically telegraphed Washington, "My report today is of deplorable importance. Chickamauga is as fatal a name in our history as Bull Run."

Chapter 7: The Rock of Chickamauga

By about 1:00, Longstreet's men had pushed almost all of McCook's XX Corps and Crittenden's XXI Corps off the field, including the commanding general Rosecrans along with them. As the commander and his routed Union soldiers began a panicked retreat toward Chattanooga, Longstreet met with Bragg, and according to Longstreet the commanding general was indecisive at best:

"After caring for and sending him off, and before we were through with our lunch, General Bragg sent for me. He was some little distance in rear of our new position. The change of the order of battle was explained, and the necessity under which it came to be made. We had taken some thirty or more field-pieces and a large number of small-arms, and thought that we had cut off and put to disorder the Twentieth and Twenty-first Corps that had retreated through the pass of the Ridge by the Dry Valley road. He was informed of orders given General Johnson for my left, and General Buckner for a battery on the right. I then offered as suggestion of the way to finish our work that he abandon the plan for battle by our right wing, or hold it to defence, draw off a force from that front that had rested since the left wing took up the battle, join them with the left wing, move swiftly down the Dry Valley road, pursue the retreating forces, occupy the gaps of the Ridge behind the enemy standing before our right, and call that force to its own relief.

He was disturbed by the failure of his plan and the severe repulse of his right wing, and was little prepared to hear suggestions from subordinates for other moves or progressive work. His words, as I recall them, were: 'There is not a man in the right wing who has any fight in him.' From accounts of his former operations I was prepared for halting work, but this, when the battle was at its tide and in partial success, was a little surprising. His humor, however, was such that his subordinate was at a loss for a reopening of the discussion. He did not wait, nor did he express approval or disapproval of the operations of the left wing, but rode for his Headquarters at Reed's Bridge.

There was nothing for the left wing to do but work along as best it could. The right wing ceased its active battle as the left forced the enemy's right centre, and the account of the commanding general was such as to give little hope of his active use of it in supporting us. After his lunch, General Johnson was ordered to make ready his own and Hindman's brigades, to see that those of Hood's were in just connection with his right, and await the opening of our battery. Preston's division was pulled away from its mooring on the river bank to reinforce our worn battle. "

Longstreet was beside himself at Bragg's suggestion that the battle was not being won, but Bragg was (correctly) disappointed that his ability to destroy the entire Army of the Cumberland was out of reach because his right wing's inability to advance allowed them to flee toward Chattanooga. With Bragg all but refusing to order anything out of his right wing, the work was left for Longstreet's men to try to finish the job against Thomas's Corps, which still held its defensive line.

By now, Longstreet's attack was hours old, and even if the terrain had allowed his general officers to see their entire commands, the ensuing pursuits and chaos had broken down a lot of coordination. D.H. Hill noted how unique it was that Thomas and Longstreet had become the de facto commanding generals on the field, writing "Some of the severest fighting had yet to be done after 3 P. M. It probably never happened before for a great battle to be fought to its bloody conclusion with the commanders of each side away from the field of conflict. But the Federals were in the hands of the indomitable Thomas, and the Confederates were under their two heroic wing commanders Longstreet and Polk."

While Thomas's corps held the same lines from the morning, Thomas had been going about ordering the impromptu line on Horseshoe Ridge, which was attracting small pockets of Union soldiers and allowing them to reform there. Brannan's division began forming on the ridge, while Negley's division went about directing artillery. While some Union generals, like corps commander Crittenden, declined to stick around, others like Phil Sheridan found their way to Horseshoe Ridge to take part in the defensive stand. Thomas's line was also bolstered by Gordon Granger's Reserve Corps; after listening to gunfire for hours and receiving no orders from the absent Rosecrans, Granger took it upon himself to march to the sound and somehow managed to march past Forrest's cavalry. Longstreet would later complain that he was not even informed of Granger's arrival by anyone on the right of the Confederate army.

Eventually, Longstreet's advance on the right compelled Thomas to move the rest of his defensive line gradually back toward Horseshoe Ridge. Longstreet explained:

"We were pushed back through the valley and up the slope, until General Preston succeeded in getting his brigade under Trigg to the support. Our battery got up at last under Major Williams and opened its destructive fire from eleven guns, which presently convinced General Thomas that his position was no longer tenable. He drew Reynolds's division from its trenches near the angle, for assignment as rearguard. Lieutenant-Colonel Sorrel, of the staff, reported this move, and was sent with orders to General Stewart to strike down against the enemy's moving forces. It seems that at the same time Liddell's division of the extreme right of our right wing was ordered against the march of the reserves. Stewart got into part of Reynolds's line and took several hundred prisoners. Meanwhile, Reynolds was used in meeting the attack and driving back the division of General Liddell. That accomplished, he was ordered to position to cover the retreat. As no reports came to the left from the commanding general or from the right wing, the repulse of Liddell's division was thought to indicate the strong holding of the enemy along his intrenched front line, and I thought that we should wait to finish the battle on the morrow."

It was only after the battle that Longstreet learned that the line he thought was strongly entrenched was actually empty, which only made him more disgusted with Bragg: "It is hardly possible that the Confederate commander could have failed to find the enemy's empty lines along the front of his right wing, and called both wings into a grand final sweep of the field to the capture of Thomas's command; but he was not present, and the condition of affairs was embarrassing to the subordinate commanders."

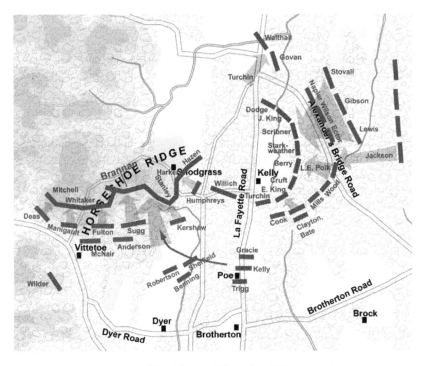

The defense of Horseshoe Ridge

Now that Thomas had all of his men back on Horseshoe Ridge, they and the scattered remnants of the other two corps who had not fled made a defiant last stand against multiple Confederate attacks. Thomas reported:

"About 2 p.m., very soon after Captain Kellogg left me, hearing heavy firing to my right and rear through the woods, I turned in that direction and was riding to the slope of the hill in my rear to ascertain the cause. Just as I passed out of the woods bordering the State road, I met Captain Kellogg returning, who reported to me that in attempting to reach General Sheridan he had met a large force in an open corn-field to the rear of Reynolds' position, advancing cautiously, with a strong line of skirmishers thrown out to their front, and that they had fired on him and forced him to return. He had reported this to Colonel Harker, commanding a brigade of Wood's division, posted on a ridge a short distance to the rear of Reynolds' position, who also saw this force advancing, but, with Captain Kellogg, was of the opinion that they might be Sheridan's troops coming to our assistance. I rode forward to Colonel Harker's position, and told him that, although I was expecting Sheridan from that direction, if those troops fired on him, seeing his flag, he must return their fire and resist their farther advance. He immediately ordered his skirmishers to commence firing, and took up a position with his brigade on the crest of a hill a short distance to his right and rear, placing his right in connection with Brannan's division and portions of Beatty's and Stanley's brigades of Negley's division, which had been retired to that point from the left, as circumstantially narrated in the reports of General John Beatty and Colonel Stanley. I then rode to the crest of the hill referred to above. On my way I met General Wood, who confirmed me in the opinion that the troops advancing upon us were the enemy, although we were not then aware of the disaster to the right and center of our army. I then directed him to place his division on the prolongation of Brannan's, who, I had ascertained from Wood, was on the top of the hill above referred to, and to resist the farther advance of the enemy as long as possible. I sent my aide, Captain Kellogg, to notify General Reynolds that our right had been turned, and that the enemy was in his rear in force.

General Wood barely had time to dispose his troops on the left of Brannan before another of those fierce assaults, similar to those made in the morning on my lines, was made on him and Brannan combined, and kept up by the enemy throwing in fresh troops as fast as those in their front were driven back, until near nightfall. About the time that Wood took up his position, General Gordon Granger appeared on my left flank at the head of Steedman's division of his corps. I immediately dispatched a staff officer, Captain Johnson, Second Indiana Cavalry, of Negley's division, to him with orders to push forward and take position on Brannan's right, which order was complied with with the greatest promptness and alacrity. Steedman, moving his division into position with almost as much precision as if on drill, and fighting his way to the crest of the hill on Brannan s right, moved forward his artillery and drove the enemy down the southern slope, inflicting on him a most terrible loss in killed and wounded. This opportune arrival of fresh troops revived the flagging spirits of our men on the right, and inspired them with new ardor for the contest. Every assault of the enemy from that time until nightfall was repulsed in the most gallant style by the whole line."

One of Rosecrans's staff officers, James Garfield, met Thomas during the afternoon, and he informed Rosecrans, "Thomas is standing like a rock." After meeting with Thomas, Garfield went so far as to suggest that Rosecrans return to the field and bring back the rest of the army to take up the fight again tomorrow, insisting "our men not only held their ground, but in many points drove the enemy splendidly. Longstreet's Virginians have got their bellies full." But Rosecrans was a beaten man, with one account claiming that he was found weeping in Chattanooga that night. Lincoln telegraphed the commanding general, "Be of good cheer. ... We have unabated confidence in you and your soldiers and officers. In the main, you must be the judge as to what is to be done. If I was to suggest, I would say save your army by taking strong positions until Burnside joins you." Lincoln, of course, knew what was truly going on, and he confided to his secretary that Rosecrans seemed "confused and stunned like a duck hit on the head."

As night fell, Thomas was able to extricate the rest of the Union defenders to Rossville Gap nearer Chattanooga right from under the nose of Bragg's army. Phil Sheridan recounted seeing Thomas near Rossville Gap that night and noted how physically and mentally exhausted he seemed:

"The General appeared very much exhausted, seemed to forget what he had stopped for, and said little or nothing of the incidents of the day. This was the second occasion on which I had met him in the midst of misfortune, for during the fight in the cedars at Stone River, when our prospects were most disheartening, we held a brief conversation respecting the line he was then taking up for the purpose of helping me. At other times, in periods of inactivity, I saw but little of him. He impressed me now as he did in the cedars, his quiet, unobtrusive demeanor communicating a gloomy rather than a hopeful view of the situation. This apparent depression was due no doubt to the severe trial through which he had gone in the last fortyeight hours, which strain had exhausted him very much both physically and mentally. His success in maintaining his ground was undoubtedly largely influenced by the fact that two-thirds of the National forces had been sent to his succor, but his firm purpose to save the army was the main-stay on which all relied after Rosecrans left the field. As the command was getting pretty well past, I rose to go in order to put my troops into camp. This aroused the General, when, remarking that he had a little flask of brandy in his saddle-holster, he added that he had just stopped for the purpose of offering me a drink, as he knew I must be very tired. He requested one of his staff-officers to get the flask, and after taking a sip himself, passed it to me. Refreshed by the brandy, I mounted and rode off to supervise the encamping of my division, by no means an easy task considering the darkness, and the confusion that existed among the troops that had preceded us into Rossville."

Thomas, on the other hand, had just earned the eternal nickname "The Rock of Chickamauga". While there is a never ending stream of acclaim going to generals like Grant, Lee, and Sherman, General Thomas has managed to fly under the radar, despite having an unusual background as a Southerner fighting for the Union and scoring almost inconceivable successes at Missionary Ridge, Franklin, and Nashville. Thomas also skillfully fought at Perryville, Stones River, and in Sherman's Atlanta Campaign, but he has remained best known for his defense at Chickamauga on September 20, 1863.

Thomas had one of the most stellar records of any officer in the war, was instrumental in the Union's ultimate victory in the Western theater, and scored the kinds of decisive victories that eluded more celebrated generals like Lee. So why does Thomas fly under the radar? A stern military man, Thomas eschewed self-promotion and aggrandizement, and though his methodical generalship was almost always successful, it sometimes annoyed General Ulysses S. Grant. With Grant's star rising as his relationship with Thomas was cooling, Thomas was on the wrong end of history. And when he died in 1870, Thomas had burned his papers and had not written memoirs or an account of his participation in the war, missing his final opportunity to directly leave his mark and define his own legacy instead of having others write it for him.

Chapter 8: The Aftermath of Chickamauga

The Battle of Chickamauga was the second deadliest battle of the Civil War with nearly 35,000 total casualties. The Army of the Cumberland had lost over 16,000, including nearly 5,000 being captured as a result of the panic of the 20th. Bragg's army lost even more, with 2,300 killed and over 14,500 wounded, losing nearly 18,500 all told. The casualties amounted to nearly 40% of both armies, a staggering number.

Like Longstreet, D.H. Hill was shocked that Bragg had no plans to pursue Rosecrans on the 21st:

"Whatever blunders each of us in authority committed before the battles of the 19th and 20th, and during their progress, the great blunder of all was that of not pursuing the enemy on the 21st. The day was spent in burying the dead and gathering up captured stores. Forrest, with his usual promptness, was early in the saddle, and saw that the retreat was a rout. Disorganized masses of men were hurrying to the rear ; batteries of artillery were inextricably mixed with trains of wagons ; disorder and confusion pervaded the broken ranks struggling to get on. Forrest sent back word to Bragg that 'every hour was worth a thousand men.' But the commander-in-chief did not know of the victory until the morning of the 21st, and then he did not order a pursuit. Rosecrans spent the day and the night of the 21st in hurrying his trains out of town. A breathing-space was allowed him; the panic among his troops subsided, and Chattanooga - the objective point of the campaign - was held."

The day after Chickamauga ended, Rosecrans put his men to work digging defensive entrenchments around Chattanooga and waiting for Washington to send reinforcements. On September 23, Bragg's army arrived at the outskirts of Chattanooga and proceeded to seize control of the surrounding heights: Missionary Ridge (to the east), Lookout Mountain (to the southwest), and Raccoon Mountain (to the west). From these key vantage points, the Confederates could not only lob long-range artillery onto the Union entrenchments but also sweep the rail and river routes that supplied the Union army. Bragg planned to lay siege to the city and starve the Union forces into surrendering.

On September 29, U. S. Secretary of War Edwin M. Stanton ordered Union general Ulysses S. Grant, commander of the newly-created Military Division of the Mississippi, to go to Chattanooga to bring all the territory from the Appalachian Mountains to the Mississippi River (including a portion of Arkansas) under a single command for the first time. Considering General Rosecrans's spotty record, Grant was given the option of replacing him with General Thomas. Hearing an inaccurate report that Rosecrans was preparing to abandon Chattanooga, Grant relieved Rosecrans of command and installed Thomas as commander of the Army of the Cumberland, telegraphing Thomas saying, "Hold Chattanooga at all hazards. I will be there as soon as possible." Without hesitation, Thomas replied, "We will hold the town till we starve."[1]

What followed were some of the most amazing operations of the Civil War. Grant relieved Rosecrans and personally came to Chattanooga to oversee the effort, placing General Thomas in charge of reorganizing the Army of the Cumberland. Meanwhile, Lincoln detached General Hooker and two divisions from the Army of the Potomac and sent them west to reinforce the garrison at Chattanooga. During a maneuver in which General Hooker had moved three divisions into Chattanooga Valley hoping to occupy Rossville Gap, Hooker's first obstacle was to bypass an artillery line the Confederates had established to block the movement of Union supplies. Initially, Grant merely used Hooker's men to establish the "Cracker Line", a makeshift supply line that moved food and resources into Chattanooga from Hooker's position on Lookout Mountain.

In November 1863, the situation at Chattanooga was dire enough that Grant took the offensive in an attempt to lift the siege. By now the Confederates were holding important high ground at positions like Lookout Mountain and Missionary Ridge. First Grant ordered General Sherman and four divisions of his Army of the Tennessee to attack Bragg's right flank, but the attempt was unsuccessful. Then, in an attempt to make an all out push, Grant ordered all forces in the vicinity to make an attack on Bragg's men.

On November 24, 1863 Maj. Gen. Hooker captured Lookout Mountain in order to divert some of Bragg's men away from their commanding position on Missionary Ridge. But the victory is best remembered for the almost miraculous attack on Missionary Ridge by part of General Thomas's Army of the Cumberland.

General Sheridan was part of a force sent to attack the Confederate midsection at nearby Missionary Ridge. According to several present, when Sheridan reached the base of Ridge, he stopped and toasted the Confederate gunners, shouting out, "Here's to you!"[2] In response, the Confederates sprayed his men with bullets, prompting Sheridan to quip, "That was ungenerous! I'll take your guns for that!" at which time he lit out, leading a spirited charge while screaming, "Chickamauga! Chickamauga!". The advance actually defied Grant's orders, since Grant,

---

[1]   Cleaves, Freeman. *Rock of Chickamauga: The Life of General George H. Thomas*. Page 182.

[2]   Gaffney, P., and D. Gaffney. *The Civil War: Exploring History One Week at a Time*. Page 308.

initially upset, had only ordered them to take the rifle pits at the base of Missionary Ridge, figuring that a frontal assault on that position would be futile and fatal. As Sheridan stormed ahead, General Grant caught the advance from a distance and asked General Thomas why he had ordered the attack. Thomas informed Grant that he hadn't; his army had taken it upon itself to charge up the entire ridge.

As it turned out, historians have often criticized Grant's orders, with acclaimed historian Peter Cozzens noting, "Grant's order to halt at the rifle pits at the base of the ridge was misunderstood by far too many of the generals charged with executing it. Some doubted the order because they thought it absurd to stop an attack at the instant when the attackers would be most vulnerable to fire from the crest and to a counterattack. Others apparently received garbled versions of the order." Sheridan later wrote, "Seeing the enemy thus strengthening himself, it was plain that we would have to act quickly if we expected to accomplish much, and I already began to doubt the feasibility of our remaining in the first line of rifle-pits when we should have carried them. I discussed the order with Wagner, Harker, and Sherman, and they were similarly impressed, so while anxiously awaiting the signal I sent Captain Ransom of my staff to Granger, who was at Fort Wood, to ascertain if we were to carry the first line or the ridge beyond. Shortly after Ransom started the signal guns were fired, and I told my brigade commanders to go for the ridge."

Regardless, to the amazement of Grant and the officers watching, the men making the attack scrambled up Missionary Ridge in a series of disorganized attacks that somehow managed to send the Confederates into a rout, thereby lifting the siege on Chattanooga. With that, the Army of the Cumberland had essentially conducted the most successful frontal assault of the war spontaneously. While Pickett's Charge, still the most famous attack of the war, was one unsuccessful charge, the Army of the Cumberland made over a dozen charges up Missionary Ridge and ultimately succeeded.

When the siege of Chattanooga was lifted, the Confederate victory at Chickamauga, the biggest battle in the Western Theater, had been rendered virtually meaningless. Not surprisingly, in the wake of Chickamauga there were recriminations among the generals involved on both sides. Chickamauga ensured Thomas continued to lead the Army of the Cumberland for the rest of the war, while the tension between Bragg and his principal subordinates bordered on outright mutiny. Longstreet discussed the unbelievable sequence of events within the Army of Tennessee's high command over the next month:

"After moving from Virginia to try to relieve our comrades of the Army of Tennessee, we thought that we had cause to complain that the fruits of our labor had been lost, but it soon became manifest that the superior officers of that army themselves felt as much aggrieved as we at the halting policy of their chief, and were calling in letters and petitions for his removal. A number of them came to have me write the

President for them. As he had not called for my opinion on military affairs since the Johnston conference of 1862, I could not take that liberty, but promised to write to the Secretary of War and to General Lee, who I thought could excuse me under the strained condition of affairs. About the same time they framed and forwarded to the President a petition praying for relief.2 It was written by General D. H. Hill (as he informed me since the war).

While the superior officers were asking for relief, the Confederate commander was busy looking along his lines for victims. Lieutenant-General Polk was put under charges for failing to open the battle of the 20th at daylight; Major-General Hindman was relieved under charges for conduct before the battle, when his conduct of the battle with other commanders would have relieved him of any previous misconduct, according to the customs of war, and pursuit of others was getting warm.

On the Union side the Washington authorities thought vindication important, and Major-Generals McCook and Crittenden, of the Twentieth and Twenty-first Corps, were relieved and went before a Court of Inquiry; also one of the generals of division of the Fourteenth Corps.

The President came to us on the 9th of October and called the commanders of the army to meet him at General Bragg's office. After some talk, in the presence of General Bragg, he made known the object of the call, and asked the generals, in turn, their opinion of their commanding officer, beginning with myself. It seemed rather a stretch of authority, even with a President, and I gave an evasive answer and made an effort to turn the channel of thought, but he would not be satisfied, and got back to his question. The condition of the army was briefly referred to, and the failure to make an effort to get the fruits of our success, when the opinion was given, in substance, that our commander could be of greater service elsewhere than at the head of the Army of Tennessee. Major-General Buckner was called, and gave opinion somewhat similar. So did Major-General Cheatham, who was then commanding the corps recently commanded by Lieutenant-General Polk, and General D. H. Hill, who was called last, agreed with emphasis to the views expressed by others."

The problem for the Confederates who wanted to be done with Bragg is that he was friends with Jefferson Davis, as Longstreet was reminded when suggesting to Davis that Bragg be replaced by Joseph E. Johnston:

"In my judgment our last opportunity was lost when we failed to follow the success at Chickamauga, and capture or disperse the Union army, and it could not be just to the service or myself to call me to a position of such responsibility. The army was part of General Joseph E. Johnston's department, and could only be used in strong organization by him in combining its operations with his other forces in Alabama and Mississippi. I said that under him I could cheerfully work in any position. The suggestion of that name only served to increase his displeasure, and his severe rebuke.

I recognized the authority of his high position, but called to his mind that neither his words nor his manner were so impressive as the dissolving scenes that foreshadowed the dreadful end. He referred to his worry and troubles with politicians and non-combatants. In that connection, I suggested that all that the people asked for was success; with that the talk of politicians would be as spiders' webs before him."

Despite the negative feelings so many held about Bragg, Davis would not relieve him of command until late November 1863, well after the disastrous siege of Chattanooga was finished. By then, Bragg had successfully suspended Hindman and Polk for what he considered to be their failures during the Chickamauga campaign, and D.H. Hill was also suspended in early October.

With the failure to make anything out of the victory at Chickamauga, the Confederacy's best chance at somehow turning the tide in the West and possibly winning the war had been lost. As a result, Chickamauga became an extremely sore subject among the Confederates who had fought there, and historians still look at it as the South's last best chance in that theater.

D.H. Hill, who had played such a controversial role in the campaign, may have put it best:

There was no more splendid fighting in '61, when the flower of the Southern youth was in the field, than was displayed in those bloody days of September, '63. But it seems to me that the élan of the Southern soldier was never seen after Chickamauga - that brilliant dash which had distinguished him was gone forever. He was too intelligent not to know that the cutting in two of Georgia meant death to all his hopes. He knew that Longstreet's absence was imperiling Lee's safety, and that what had to be done must be done quickly. The delay in striking was exasperating to him; the failure to strike after the success was crushing to all his longings for an independent South. He fought stoutly to the last, but, after Chickamauga, with the sullenness of despair and without the enthusiasm of hope.

That 'barren victory' sealed the fate of the Southern Confederacy."

Bibliography

Cleaves, Freeman. Rock of Chickamauga: The Life of General George H. Thomas. Norman: University of Oklahoma Press, 1948.

Connelly, Thomas L. Autumn of Glory: The Army of Tennessee 1862–1865. Baton Rouge: Louisiana State University Press, 1971.

Cozzens, Peter. This Terrible Sound: The Battle of Chickamauga. Urbana: University of Illinois

Press, 1992.

Knudsen, LTC Harold M. General James Longstreet: The Confederacy's Most Modern General. Tarentum, PA: Word Association Publishers, 2007.

Korn, Jerry, and the Editors of Time-Life Books. The Fight for Chattanooga: Chickamauga to Missionary Ridge. Alexandria, VA: Time-Life Books, 1985.

Lamers, William M. The Edge of Glory: A Biography of General William S. Rosecrans, U.S.A. Baton Rouge: Louisiana State University Press, 1961.

Tucker, Glenn. Chickamauga: Bloody Battle in the West. Dayton, OH: Morningside House, 1972.

Turchin, John Basil. Chickamauga. Chicago: Fergus Printing Co., 1888.

U.S. War Department, The War of the Rebellion: a Compilation of the Official Records of the Union and Confederate Armies. Washington, DC: U.S. Government Printing Office, 1880–1901.

Welsh, Douglas. The Civil War: A Complete Military History. Greenwich, CT: Brompton Books Corporation, 1981.

Woodworth, Steven E. Six Armies in Tennessee: The Chickamauga and Chattanooga Campaigns. Lincoln: University of Nebraska Press, 1998.

Made in the USA
Middletown, DE
03 September 2020